Praise for *Unmothered*

Honest, open, and authentic, Phylis Mantelli gives the reader an in-depth look at motherhood from her vulnerable childhood with her own unstable mother, to adulthood, marriage, and becoming a mother to her own children. In *Unmothered*, the reader will learn how she coped and how God helped her find peace. Mantelli's work shines with strength, determination, and commitment.

—B. J. Taylor, *Guideposts* writer and novelist

With grit and grace, Phylis Mantelli draws you into her journey of mothering while unmothered. Mantelli tends to the parent wound in her readers, while cultivating a deeper appreciation for those we love. She exemplifies how forgiving the unforgiveable and loving the unlovable leads to a prosperous and fulfilling life. Teens, parents, and grandparents alike will encounter healing within their hearts and families after reading this redemptive story.

—Cherie Denna, writer and blogger
Leader of women's ministries at Life Community Church

This beautiful book is about restoration and how generational curses can be broken. Phylis is honest and vulnerable in her story about her dysfunctional relationship with her mother. She explains how God's love and grace gave her a chance to change the next generation. No matter what your relationship is with your mom, this book will inspire you to break those generational chains that so often bind us.

—Rhonda Velez, writer and counselor
Cohost of the podcast *24 Carat Conversations with Phylis & Rhonda*

Phylis Mantelli's memoir reads like a movie script. You're quickly turning pages to see what's going to happen next. In a refreshingly honest and vulnerable look into her own demons, Phylis shares her tenuous relationship with a mother looking for love without knowing how to love. Phylis bravely learned that you don't have to repeat the past when you let God guide your future. *Unmothered* is a must read for anyone who struggles with a troubled mother-daughter dynamic. I wish I had read a book like this when my own mother and I were estranged for years. I know Phylis's compassion, insight, and wisdom will encourage many mothers and daughters to let God help them work through their issues, even if there's only one trying.

—Janet Thompson, speaker and author of twenty books, including
Everyday Brave: Living Courageously as a Woman of Faith and
Mentoring for All Seasons: Sharing Life Experiences and God's Faithfulness

Unmothered

LIFE WITH A MOM
Who Couldn't Love Me

PHYLIS MANTELLI

Unmothered

LIFE WITH A MOM
Who Couldn't Love Me

REDEMPTION
PRESS

Published by Redemption Press, PO Box 427, Enumclaw, WA 98022

Toll Free (844) 2REDEEM (273-3336)

Redemption Press is honored to present this title in partnership with the author. The views expressed or implied in this work are those of the author. Redemption Press provides our imprint seal representing design excellence, creative content, and high quality production.

The author has tried to recreate events, locales, and conversations from her memories of them. In order to maintain their anonymity, in some instances she has changed the names of individuals and may have changed some identifying characteristics and details, such as physical properties, occupations, and places of residence.

ISBN 13: 978-1-68314-740-4 (Paperback)
978-1-68314-741-1 (ePub)
978-1-68314-742-8 (Mobi)

Library of Congress Catalog Card Number: 2019909482

To my grandson, Koston, who makes me believe in future generations.

Contents

Foreword

FOR OVER TWENTY-FIVE YEARS, I'VE been ministering to women who have felt oh so broken in a myriad of ways. Due to the nature of my books on sexuality and healthy relationships, it's often a troubled marriage or a pattern of rocky relationships that brings them to me for individual or couple's coaching, and many will attend one of my Women at the Well four-day intensive workshops.

Leading these workshops has revealed an interesting phenomenon. I assumed when I started them almost ten years ago that I would attract lots of women with "daddy issues." Maybe they grew up without a father in the home because of divorce, or their dad was emotionally volatile or physically or sexually abusive, and this caused them to shut down sexually or emotionally or to "look for love in all the wrong places," as the country song declares.

However, almost forty workshops later, I've realized that yes, absent or abusive daddies can do a lot of damage to their daughter's spirit. But the participants with the deepest self-esteem struggles and darkest secrets they're exhausted from trying to hide are often dealing with an entirely different paradigm—they struggle with "mama trauma."

Could there ever be a more important person, a more identity-shaping figure in our lives than our mothers? They carry us in their wombs and labor to bring us into the world. They fill our bellies with enough milk or formula to satiate us and help us grow into independent beings. They teach us how to talk, relate, bond, connect, and the list goes on and on. They are our mirrors for the first two decades of our lives! What we think of ourselves, we glean from what we perceive Mama thinks of us.

But what if Mama's mental/emotional mirror is distorted, like a funhouse mirror that exaggerates certain features and ultimately isn't flattering at all? It can seem like an overwhelming task to view yourself through any lens other than the one Mama held up—a task that many women invest a lifetime of energy attempting to master.

For example, Candace came to a workshop in her midthirties. Her mother struggled with obsessive-compulsive disorder and a severe case of germophobia. "The sight of dirt, spit, snot, blood, or vomit sent Mama reeling with anxiety and fear," Candace explained to the group. "If I had a runny nose, or scraped my knee, or had an upset stomach, I knew better than to expect my mom to do anything about it but freak out and scream at me. So I hid every ailment, hoping she'd be more accepting of me. But I was never clean enough, groomed enough, well enough to earn a place anywhere close to her side. It's like she had an invisible shield of protection around her, and I wasn't welcome inside that circle."

As you can imagine, Candace grew up longing for a loving mother figure and leaned heavily on every strong, accepting female teacher or mentor she could find. Unfortunately, she exhausted some of these women, who viewed her as clingy or codependent, and that has done a number on her self-esteem. Rather than risking rejection in real relationships, she drowns her sorrows with excessive alcohol and pornography. Her nagging insecurities scream, *Will I ever be good enough for anyone to love me?*

Roberta is another "unmothered" soul. She grew up in a home with a revolving door, as there seemed to be a steady flow of men coming in, but always going out too. They'd stay awhile and make promises to take care of her and her mother, but those promises were always broken. When Roberta was in her late teens, she figured out the reason. Behind her mother's beautiful porcelain-doll face and lustrous brunette hair was a soul tormented by bouts of deep, debilitating depression. She would remain in bed for days without showering or eating much. Roberta would get herself ready for school, make her own breakfast, lunch, and dinner, and take care of most of the household chores. She had little time for socializing with friends and was too embarrassed to bring boyfriends home for fear they would run away like her mother's boyfriends always did. When Roberta left for college, her mother drank lawn poison and took her own life. Now in her sixties, Roberta has wrestled with this question for over forty years: "Why wasn't I enough to give my mother a reason to live?"

I'm so grateful to have been given a glimpse into these women's lives and to have the opportunity to create a group workshop experience for them to ease some of the painful burdens they've carried. Often some of these women would ask, "I know you have books on overcoming daddy issues, but do you have one *for me* and my mommy issues?" However, I felt ill equipped to ever attempt such a book in light of the fact that my mom had been a strong, supportive figure in my life.

So imagine my delight when I met Phylis Mantelli and she told me of her vision to write the book you're holding in your hands. Phylis signed up for my B.L.A.S.T. Mentorship program in 2017, and I've been incredibly honored to cheer her on through the process of finalizing this book and getting it ready to minister to the masses who know all too well the sting of rejection from the very people who are supposed to teach us what unconditional love and acceptance should feel like.

Phylis attended a special live event that I hosted for writers and speakers and took the stage to share parts of her personal story that drove her in this direction with her ministry. The audience was captivated by her courage and offered to rally around her efforts to make this message available in book form. I know it's going to have the same effect on you. You're going to fall in love with Phylis, celebrate her courage, cherish her authenticity, and catch the vision that just because a parent fails us doesn't mean that we have to be failure ourselves. Phylis has a phenomenal relationship with her own children, and she is a refreshing reminder that *we* choose our own destiny. *We* determine what legacy we leave behind. *We* can find purpose in our pain, by first allowing God to be the healer of our souls, and then by allowing God to use our story for His glory.

I pray you feel the motherly warmth in these pages, sense sweet hugs in Phylis's words of wisdom, and recognize the love in her heart toward *you*, dear reader. And that you, in turn, are able to love others well as a result of reading this book.

Shannon Ethridge
MA life/relationship coach, speaker and author of twenty-two books, including the million-copy best-selling Every Woman's Battle series

Acknowledgments

THERE ARE SO MANY TO thank on this page—all who helped my dream come true and became an advocate for all the "unmothered."

To my husband, Mike—thank you for your constant love, belief, and support of me throughout the years. I love you forever. My two beautiful, talented daughters, Ariel and Dominique—thank you for helping me with all things technical and giving me the encouragement to tell my truth. You are both the best part of me. To the best son-in-law, Julius. You have added much joy to our family. I love you so much. You and Ariel gave me the best gift—my grandson, Koston. You are my heart.

Without the support of New Hope Community Church, I never would have had a voice to share my story. Special thanks to my pastor, Malcolm MacPhail, and his beautiful wife, Kathy. You always inspire me and keep me faithful in listening to God's voice.

To my amazing prayer warriors, Rhonda Velez, Lorraine Martinez, Debbie Shrull, Nicole Del Moral, Stefanie Wambgans-Rodriquez, and Piper Pluckhan—you shared my tears and frustrations of getting this written and kept praying me through it.

To my small-group gals on Wednesday nights at church—I am grateful for your hearts. To my first-ever writing group, the wonderful women of Gilroy who encouraged me to start writing and never stop. We met every week over ten years ago, but our bond and friendships remain. To the original crew—J. Chris Mickartz, Karen LaCorte, Linda Estill, and the late Kathleen Smith. The moments we spent talking, eating, and laughing at all our ideas are priceless. The reading of our stories and what we had written (or not) for the week was more of a bonding and support than you will ever know.

To Laura Wrede, the woman who led me to Mount Hermon—your encouragement to improve my writing skills there led me to finding my writing voice. I will be forever grateful.

To my Mount Hermon forever friends—I love you more than words can say. Special thanks to my mentors over the years: B. J. Taylor, my first mentor/teacher who told me I was a great writer—you were the first one to ever read my work. Janet Thompson, Jeannette Hanscome, and many others too numerous to say—I so appreciate your encouragement. My many friends I met there—Cherie Denna, Jennifer Baker, Penny Penrod, Gabriela Banks, Crystal Hodges Johnson—you have become some of my closest friends and writing advocates.

Anna Vatuone, you are my social media guru. Thank you for always meeting with me to update all things marketing and for listening to my confusing mind. Thank you for being a part of my team. More than that, you are the sweetest person and a friend.

To Shannon Ethridge, my B.L.A.S.T. life coach. You have shown me strength and confidence that I wouldn't have had without your program and leadership. You are a wonderful teacher and friend. I must also give a shout-out to my fellow BLASTERS Nicki Bradshaw, Alecia Davis, Tamara Lewis, Carol Larson, Denise Mast Broadwater, Dena Johnson Martin, Loyla Louvis, and Laura White—I love you all.

To the best publishing company ever, Redemption Press. To my publisher, Athena Dean Holtz—thank you for pursuing me and always supporting me. To the best managing editor, Dori Harrell—thank you for making me go deeper with my story and for supporting my goal to prayerfully help many other women. To my project manager, Hannah McKenzie—I have never met you in person, but I appreciate you. Thank you for always returning my email questions and keeping me on track.

To my siblings and dad—we are still standing through all the rough times. My prayer is that we continue to thrive and learn from our past.

To my Savior and eternal Father God, who has generously shown me a straight path through His strength and truth to break the generational chain of family dysfunction.

Introduction

YOU SEE IT EVERY DAY: mothers and daughters at lunch together or shopping at the mall, walking—sometimes hand in hand—laughing, crying, perhaps arguing, or just having a moment. Sometimes those moments become a larger part of life: mothers and daughters take vacations together, start businesses together, or move in next door.

Is that typical? I wonder. *Too much? Just enough?* What does a normal relationship between a mother and daughter look like? It took me a long time to answer because my relationship with my mom didn't look like any of that.

Mothers are supposed to be overprotective, always loving, and always there for you—at least that's what the Hallmark cards say. What if you grew up without that kind of mom?

That's my story. I didn't understand normal mother-daughter relationships. My relationship with my mom was different than what I saw in others because it lacked intimacy, involvement, or any concern for my well-being. I grew up feeling empty, alone, and hurt, and because of it, I wondered, *Am I damaged goods that can never heal?*

Conflicts between mothers and daughters are classic. There are volumes written on the subject. Psychologists have tried to describe why women who share common DNA have relationship challenges. The relationship I had with my mom had many common problems, communication being one of them. She never saw me as an individual with my own passions and goals. I had to agree with her on everything, or I was against her. This was also compounded by her long-term alcohol abuse. Her continuing up-and-down mood swings temporarily subsided when she had a night out drinking. It released the anxiety that stirred within her.

She, however, became my abuser. Not my protector. Not my confidant. Not my shopping buddy or carpool driver or even someone to hug me when I cried. In her drunken state, she put me in harm's way with strangers. Her problems drove us apart. Then through a painful but ultimately liberating journey with a God who loves us, we were brought back together.

Someone once told me a vital step to healing is forgiveness. Could I find it in my heart to forgive this woman who was never available emotionally or physically? How could I overcome the years of neglect and abuse?

From the dark corners of an abusive childhood, God gave me an extraordinary opportunity to learn about patience, grace, and redemption in my own life. I became my mom's caretaker in her final years. Through those years I came away with six life lessons. They have freed me to finally live a life full of joy.

I'm not a therapist (although I confer with them for their expertise when needed). I'm a woman who wants to help others who may not have the kind of a mom they can turn to when they need help. I am a mentor mama who wants to share my journey.

If you find your story somewhere in the pages of this book, you will know that your past doesn't have to define your future, because there is hope and healing and a brighter tomorrow. You deserve the family God has planned for you. This will take some hard work on your part. I have often said, "You can't change generational dysfunction until you change the dysfunction in you."

You have learned some bad habits that may seem normal to you. You have grown up in a faulty environment. If you are ready to make changes so you can move forward, it may mean leaving some old habits behind. It may mean leaving behind some people who aren't healthy for you anymore. If you want to live your best life now, keep reading my story. May my story guide you, and perhaps my struggle, and what I ultimately left behind, will be similar to your story. And I pray that God will speak to you through these pages and lead you to a clear path of a vibrant, blessed, victorious life.

CHAPTER 1

Where Is Home?

I DIDN'T KNOW WHAT WOULD happen when I saw my mom, but I was happy, for a change, because I was walking home with a new friend and neighbor. My older brother, Brian, dragged his feet behind us.

As we strolled to my house, I saw a huge semi-truck parked at the curb. Two men carried out our couch and loaded it onto the truck. Fear rose in me. What was going on? Something bad would happen when I stepped through my front door. That was how it was in our home—always something surprising, and mostly scary.

"Why is there a truck in front of your house?" my new friend asked.

I didn't have an answer.

I left my friend at the curb and ran toward the front door, my brother right behind me, only to stop dead in my tracks when I reached the living room. Every room was empty! My mother gave orders to the men carrying the last items to go into the truck, rushing them as if she were late for a meeting. Her eyes caught mine but quickly darted back to the movers.

Dizzy, I tried to catch my breath. My eight-year-old brain could only handle so much. *Where are we going? Where is our stuff? Where is Daddy? Were we moving far? Was I going to be able to see my friends? Where is my dad?*

I started to drill Mom with questions, but I only made it as far as my first one. "Is Daddy home?"

Mom was now in manic mode as my brother marched up to her. "What is going on?"

My mother looked at us with steely eyes. "We have to hurry. We're meeting someone at the park!"

Once again I asked, "Where's Daddy?"

She gritted her teeth. "He's not here. Now get your stuff and let's get going."

I knew I needed to shut up and just follow her. If I didn't, there would be a slap to the back of my head that would force the quietness back into me.

I took one last look around this wonderful house. It looked even bigger than when filled with furniture. I peeked into my parents' room. My favorite space was the big bay window. It was where I spent my time daydreaming after school. Where I waited for my daddy to come home after a long trip. But mostly, my nights were spent sitting at the vanity, getting my hair tugged and pin curled each night.

Mom grabbed a small swirl of my hair and rolled it tight to my head, securing it with two bobby pins crisscrossed on top. "Phylis Ann, I'm going to haul off and give you the biggest spanking of your life if you don't sit still!"

"Mommy, it hurts," I cried out as the next bobby pin stabbed my head.

"It's not that bad. You are so dramatic. I'm a hairdresser, for goodness' sake. I did this for a living. Stop being a sissy."

Mom loved to remind me how she used to work in a beauty parlor and knew hair better than me. My perfect hair was her pride and joy and was done up just like the movie star Shirley Temple: reddish-brown ringlets bounced against my cheeks. When the neighbors remarked about my hair, Mom's face glowed through her smile.

"Oh, Pat, your little girl looks adorable! Look at that gorgeous head of hair. Every hair in place," the neighbor said, touching my swirled, curly locks.

"Thank you! Phylis does have the most beautiful hair. Now if I can just get her to sit still while I'm curling it every night."

They laughed, looking down at me.

One day I destroyed those curls.

It was picture day at school. I wore my red dress with the white collar and blue polka-dot skinny bow tie on the front. As I walked each block closer to the classroom, I tugged at the ends of my hair to loosen those annoying ringlets. I arrived that morning with a lopsided hairdo and a red ribbon dangling by my ear.

Weeks later Mom saw the photographs and flipped out. "How could you do this to me? I paid for these already. Now I can't send them out to any of the relatives. You look horrible. I spent hours on your hair, and this is the thanks I get? You did this on purpose!" Mom screamed as she threw the pictures in a drawer, never to be sent out to anyone.

I endured the worst spanking of my life that day, and I'd run to Mom and Dad's bedroom. It was also my safe spot when Mommy was mad at Daddy. I'd hear them in the kitchen, fighting about how much he was gone for work.

"Why can't you stay home and find more local driving jobs?" she pleaded through tears.

"What do you want me to do?" Dad yelled back. I'm making money so you can live in this nice house."

"It's too hard taking care of both kids by myself all the time!" Mom screamed. "There is no one here to talk to at the end of the day. I have had enough child talk to make me throw up. I need adult time."

I'd escape to their bedroom and listen to the birds chirping. I'd let the sun warm my face and pretend I had a mom and dad who never spoke cruel words to each other.

Although we didn't always have the best of times in this house, there were times my parents were happy together, like when we took road trips to visit Grandma Rose.

Grandma Rose was my favorite person. She spoke mainly Portuguese. She would teach me Portuguese words, and I would help her with her English. She always had homemade Coke popsicles in the freezer. My grandmother would hug me tight when I walked through the door to her home in Merced, California.

"Pheeliz, come give me big hug, linda menina" (beautiful little girl). *She pulled me close to her chest.*

I loved the comfort of her arms.

I would tuck away those memories in my heart for now. Would I ever see Grandma Rose again? Or Auntie Laura and Uncle Paul?

Mom had two best friends from when she was single. One was Laura, my godmother. A working woman, Auntie Laura had married an older gentleman but had no children. Auntie Laura and Uncle Paul were the parents I pretended were mine. They had a beautiful one-story home that was open and spacious enough for kids to run around and not break anything. There was a big backyard with an even bigger pool for us to swim in during the summer. Not being such a great swimmer, I opted to sit by the pool and dangle my feet in the cool water.

But Auntie Laura's "doll room" launched me into daydreams for hours. The space was reserved for the porcelain dolls she collected from her travels. They were enclosed in wall-to-wall glass cabinets. A Dutch girl, Indian, Spanish, Swedish, each with its own dress. I'd sit on the floor and imagine what they would be like if they were human.

They would have moms who were kind to them.

Mom and Auntie Laura stood by the door and talked about the "good old days" when they were young and single. Mom seemed more relaxed, but her stress boomed loud and clear when she talked about her life.

"I wish I would have known how much work it was raising children. I miss having my freedom. And that no-good husband of mine is never home to help. I am just like a single mom." She crossed her arms with a big sigh.

"Oh, Patty girl, you are blessed with these kids." Auntie Laura glanced my way. "Look at this one. She's adorable. What I would give to have a little girl."

As I listened to their conversation, I drifted into my own world of how I would live if I were a Dutch girl like this doll. What would it be like to walk in those wooden shoes? I wondered what her country was like. Our last name, Van Winkle, was a Dutch name, so it was possible I had relatives in Holland.

Auntie Laura disrupted my thoughts. "Stay for dinner. Paul and I would love to have you all stay." She hugged my mom as they headed toward the kitchen. Finally, some alone time.

Now, as the moving men slammed the door to that huge truck, I wondered if I would ever dream in that doll room again?

As my mom bossed the movers around, I meandered from the bedroom to the kitchen, soaking in all the memories. The kitchen was big and always smelled delicious. Today it made me sad to walk in here knowing it would be the last time. An excellent cook, my mother loved making food from scratch. She had to, since only my dad worked and we lived on a strict budget. But my mother had grown up cooking this way. Her homemade bread was just the best thing coming out of the oven! We couldn't wait to smother it with butter. It dripped all over my fingers. Feeling the warmth of the bread and tasting the sweetness helped soothe the anxiety from my parents' verbal battles. And the cookies. The scent of warm dough mixed with chocolate would waft through the house. It hit your nose as soon as you walked through the door. I knew it would be a good day if Mom was baking.

There were scary times in this kitchen too. I flashbacked to when my mom had lunged at my dad with a knife.

He grabbed her hand.

She missed his body but sliced his shirt open, tearing into his skin.

Watching them, I whimpered.

"It's okay, honey. Daddy's fine," my father assured me.

I wandered into the living room. It had been filled with fluffy furniture you could sink into. Lots of antiques (which my mom loved) and tons of knickknacks everywhere (which I hated to dust!). We had to dust every one of them once or twice a week, depending on Mom's mood.

I stood where the TV had been. Mom only allowed us to watch it if she wanted to. Usually Ed Sullivan, Lawrence Welk, or Carol Burnett.

She continually said how she hated having my dad gone and being alone. Many nights she went out drinking at the bars. Since she could walk anywhere in our small town, it was easy for her to take off on any given night. Sometimes she left us alone. Other times she found teenagers or a neighbor she trusted to come watch us for a few hours.

On the nights Mom stayed home, we kids watched her favorite shows, then acted out the characters. Mom looked like Carol Burnett, so Mom imitated her. I loved Tim Conway and Vicki Lawrence. We quoted the funny lines to each other. Our laughter filled the air.

Otherwise, Mom hated TV. A stubborn Portuguese woman, she limited TV watching, and she had no phone or car.

"I can walk anywhere in this town. Why do I need to spend gas on a car? And a phone? What a stupid box that is. People look ridiculous with a clunky thing attached to their ear. Why can't they go down the street in person to talk if they have something to say?" She was proud of her reasoning.

She didn't like change. Her life was about hard work and doing things from scratch. Her immaculate house showed it.

I stood in the space in the living room where my dad's favorite flowered chair had sat. I loved sitting on his lap after he came home from a long trip.

"Who's my favorite girl?" he asked.

"Daaaad, I'm your only girl!" Giggling, I hugged him.

A drink balancing in one hand, his arms around me, he joked with me and tickled me until I slid to the floor, laughing hysterically.

My dad, Harold, called "Rip" by his friends, was a long-distance truck driver of fresh produce. I was Daddy's girl, and my mother resented this. He would bring my brother and me gifts and surprise us with them, even in the middle of the night—and the disruption of our sleep irritated my mom.

"Don't you dare wake them up now. I will never get them back to sleep," Mom whispered, loud enough that I could hear her.

"I want to see their faces when I give them this." He bolted through the bedroom door, holding a stuffed animal.

It wasn't just any stuffed animal—it was the biggest brown bear I had ever seen.

"Daddy!" I wiped the sticky gunk from my eyes.

"Hey, princess, look what Daddy brought you."

He laid the bear on me, and it was taller than I was. I gave it the biggest squeeze and then did the same to my dad.

My mom crossed her arms over her chest. She had a strained smile on her face. She tried to be happy, but I didn't think she was. "Okay, okay, that's enough excitement for tonight. Turn the lights out and go to sleep." She stomped out of the room.

My dad winked at me and smiled that warm smile of his and shut the door. And then I heard them fighting. Something about my dad never respecting her and how he ruined everything. I hugged my bear.

"Back off, Pat. I'm just trying to show my kids I love them."

Mom's real name was Ida, but she hated that name, so she went by "Pat," as her middle name was Patricia.

When my parents were together, they laughed hard and fought hard. When it turned ugly, screams echoed and fists flew. Then the cops would come and tell my dad to calm down or they would take him in.

When my dad was gone, my mom usually wound up at a bar, which was a weekly habit.

"Only alcoholics have booze in the house," she rationalized to us as she put on lipstick, preparing to leave.

She walked us to a friend's house. I loved going to Mary's. She made us scrumptious homemade tortillas, which I ate till my stomach hurt. Her house was filled with laughter, hugs, and warmth. She showered love on her children, and as Mary tucked us into bed, I pretended she was my mom.

Bedtime at my house was brush teeth, brush hair, bedtime story, quick kiss on the cheek or forehead. Mom's good-nights were filled with rushed actions. At Mary's, her good-night kisses were rounded out with a soft cuddle, some tickles and giggles, and a big kiss and a huge hug. Mary's good-nights were filled with love.

We were awakened by my mother's voice saying she had to take us home right then. Mary pleaded with her, saying it was cold outside and we shouldn't be walking home this late. She begged my mom to let us stay, but my mother insisted we leave right away.

We shivered as we marched to our house. A car sped up behind us, and I turned. It was my dad, who screeched to the curb.

He jumped out, screaming at my mom. "I saw you! Don't pretend you didn't see me tonight. What the hell are you doing out, Pat?"

She had been caught. She'd thought he would still be away for work, but he had come home early. He grabbed my mom and pushed her to the ground.

She turned around and yelled, "Run!"

We took off down the street. As we reached the end of the block, I said to my brother, "Where do we go?" We raced back toward Mom, who was running toward us, with Dad right behind her. When he approached me, he picked me up and lifted me in the air. I wasn't sure why, but I was scared, and I screamed.

It was the ammunition my mom needed. "See—she doesn't want you!"

The look on my father's face tore at my heart. He looked broken. He put me back down on the ground. The neighbors had heard the ruckus and had called the police. My mother, brother, and I were put in the back of a police car. My dad was put in handcuffs. I shook all over my body, which didn't feel like my own.

"Stop shaking! Sit still!" My mom grabbed my wobbly knees and held them down.

I didn't have control of my body. It felt like it belonged to someone else.

My dad went to jail. The three of us spent the night at a motel, for safety. None of us slept.

Something was broken in our family.

And now I stood here in my childhood home, scared, saying goodbye. We were leaving . . . without my dad.

CHAPTER 2

Life Changes Forever

THE WALK FROM OUR HOME to the park was fast paced and quiet. My mother's eyes darted in all directions, as if someone might be following us. The emotions coming from my mother frightened me. She was looking for something or someone.

We made it to the park and stood by the fun outdoor toys, watching other families play. A tan-colored car with a man in it was parked across the way. She made a beeline straight for this stranger's car while holding our hands. We'd always been told not to get into strangers' cars, but this day was different. My mother ordered us to hurry up and climb in.

I stood there in shock. My instinct told me, *Danger! Don't enter!* I looked at my mother as if she was crazy.

She raised her voice. "Get in the car now."

I reluctantly slid onto the backseat with my brother.

The man looked at me from his rearview mirror. I could only see the back of his thick jet-black hair, though his small, beady eyes stared back at me as he adjusted the mirror to get a better view of my brother and me.

"These are my children, Phylis and Brian," my mom said, her tone giddy. "Kids, this is Jerry."

"Hello," we said, sitting quietly like all good children should. Just as our mom had taught us. To be seen and not heard.

All I could think about was where my dad was and why wasn't he with us? I wondered if Mom had left him our new address. Would he be joining us soon? Somehow, I felt he wouldn't be because there was another man. I watched my mom stroke this stranger's arm and talk softly to him.

It felt as if we'd been in the car for hours when we approached a winding road. We drove up to stacks of small houses, and I started to understand why our furniture had been packed out of our house. We parked in one of those funny driveways that was open on all ends, with cars parked everywhere. It looked like a bunch of cars for sale in a lot. My mother slid out, helped me and my brother out of the backseat, and led us through a small door that opened right into the kitchen.

"This is our new home!" she announced.

As we inched farther in, I saw a compact, tiny, square living room and stairs. The walls were stark white with a fresh-paint smell. A sliding door with a dusty beige curtain went to an outdoor enclosed patio. My mind was overwhelmed as I looked around. We had never had stairs before. We ran up to see the second level.

There were two bedrooms and a bathroom. Our mother told us which room belonged to me. The spacious window in my room overlooked the city.

But there were only two bedrooms in this apartment. Where would my brother sleep?

"You'll be sharing a room," Mom said.

"What? Mom, no! We can't share a room. He's a boy." I waited for another answer.

This was awful. I'd always had my own room. And a playroom. And lots of space.

"Well, the other room is our room." She pointed at Jerry. "There are no other rooms. Don't be selfish. Who do you think you are? A princess? Maybe with your father, but not with me, young lady. You will take the room I tell you and shut your mouth before I shut it for you." Mom clomped downstairs, telling Jerry what an ungrateful child I was.

I looked at my brother. He looked away. Tears filled my eyes.

Now we knew that this strange man would be staying with us too.

I stared out the bedroom window, thinking about the home I'd just left. How I wished I could wake up again the next morning and be back in my parents' bedroom. The room where the birds chirped and I felt safe. I dreamed of how the city lights would look from this second-floor building at night. I dreamed of growing up and never having to move again.

I gazed out that window and closed my eyes, wanting to be anywhere but there.

The days in this small apartment turned into months. And Mom's belly grew bigger. She stayed at home and cooked meals every night, waiting for Jerry to come home. He had to have rice. Every morning the scent of rice drifted up to our bedroom. I didn't mind. I loved rice—and mostly the soy sauce that I drizzled on it.

There were chores every day to be done precisely and on time, which we never completed quite to her liking. Her complaints were always the same. She couldn't get the apartment clean enough. It was hard for her to relax. Sitting still was being lazy.

"Why can't you clean it right the first time? Are you guys stupid or something? Why bother going to school? You aren't learning anything." She pushed on our heads, propelling us to the spots we'd missed.

We had to eat whatever was put in front of us and eat it all. One time I didn't want to eat the disgusting peas out of the can. She told me I couldn't leave the table without eating them. I shoved the peas into my napkin when she wasn't looking, and before I washed my plate at the sink, I threw the napkin under the refrigerator. I forgot to fetch the napkin, and Mom found it when she cleaned underneath the refrigerator the next day.

"Phylis Ann, what is this?" She held the smooshed-up napkin with slimy peas in her hand and pointed at my face. "I should sit you at that table and make you eat these. Wait until Jerry gets home! You will get the beating of your life. Don't you ever try something like that again." She moved close to my face and raised her hand to smack me, then backed off.

I wished she would hit me so I could get it over with. Now I must wait until the end of the day. My stomach knotted. I'd been punished like this before. I didn't want it to happen ever again.

He walked through the door, and I heard Mom telling him what must be done. He ushered me upstairs.

In their bedroom hung a barber belt, a thick, long brown piece of leather that barbers sharpened their knives on. I wanted to hide it or throw it away forever.

"Pull your pants down. Bend over." He wrapped the belt around his hand.

"No! I don't want to. Please . . ."

Shaking, I rolled my pants to my ankles and leaned over the bed. The first *thwack* left me stunned. Then the next one struck, and it was even worse. Tears flowed down my cheeks. I screamed in pain as he hit me four more times.

Done, he tromped back downstairs. I pulled my pants up and ran to the bathroom, where I yanked my pants back down and turned around to look at the swollen red marks left on my legs and backside.

If my dad knew Jerry was smacking me with a belt, there would be trouble. My dad never hit me. I'd cried too many times trying to find out what happened to my father, but he was not to be mentioned anymore in this apartment. I knew only that he was working and would not live here. I flung myself onto my bed and sobbed tears no one would help dry.

Mom had enrolled us in a new school. I didn't like being the new kid at school, and we walked even farther to get there than we had at our other school. Being new sucked. When the teacher introduced me, everyone stared at me like some creepy science project.

The teacher politely looked at me, smiling wide. "Class, welcome our new student, Phylis. She will be joining us for this school year. Please make her feel welcome."

I wanted to crawl out the door and run back to my real home and school. Where my dad, friends, my own bedroom, and my stuff used to be. I walked back down the aisle toward a seat in the back of the room. As I passed each kid, they looked away.

No one wanted to be my friend.

I ate lunch on the bench alone that day. I watched the girls on the playground huddled together, giggling.

To make matters worse, Mom always overdressed us. On rainy days, she made sure we had rain boots, hat, raincoat, and umbrella. The cool kids didn't bundle up. They made fun of us for being bundled-up babies.

"Let's make a deal," my brother said.

Each day before school we walked through a grassy field by our home. We stashed the umbrellas, rain boots, and hats in the field and left them there, praying no one would steal them. At the end of the day, we collected them, put them on, and headed home. My stomach would be in knots all day worrying about those items. Miraculously, they were always there, and our reputation was repaired with our peers.

It was important not to draw any attention to myself. But just when I thought I fit in, my classmates branded me as an outcast.

"My mom says your mom is living with someone in sin." Joey mockingly shouted at me in the hallway.

The kids in the hallway stopped and stared in my direction.

I whipped around and looked him square in the eye. "She is not! She's married. Shut up, Joey!" I marched away, knowing I'd lied. I didn't know why it was bad not to be married. I just knew I had one more thing to be ashamed of.

A few days later, some of the boys were picking on my brother. After class my brother raced to the farthest corner of my classroom.

Puzzled, I looked toward the front door of the classroom and back at my brother. "What's wrong? What are you doing in here? I thought I was going to meet you out front."

A group of boys stood there. The leader of this pack glared at my brother. "Why don't you come out here, sissy? Are you being protected by your baby sister?" the leader said in a baby voice.

As I walked toward him, a rage rose inside me. "Why do you think it's okay to pick on someone for no reason? If you want to fight someone, fight me!" I pushed him hard, and he fell back a step.

"Whoa . . . take it easy! I'm not fighting a baby girl. Come on, guys. Let's go." He glanced back at my brother. "I'll come for you tomorrow."

My brother stalked toward me as I waited for my "thank you" from him.

"Why did you do that?" he asked, furious. "You just made it worse. Now they're gonna make fun of me even more." He stomped out of the classroom.

I hated this school, the kids, and everything about this town. I wanted to go back to my real home.

One day my mom sat us down after school. "Mommy has something to talk to you both about." She fidgeted with her dress as she sat beside us. "Do you know why my belly has been getting bigger?"

We stared at her, confused.

"Well . . . I'm going to have a baby. Which means you are going to have a little brother or sister!" She smiled, now that her secret was out.

My mind raced. *A baby? Does Dad know? When is he coming back to take care of us? Can we go back home now?*

"This is Jerry's baby. It will be your half-sibling. It will be part Japanese, Filipino, and Portuguese. You all have the same mommy. Just different daddies."

She talked faster than I could keep up with. My hands gripped the sofa as the meaning of her words flashed in my head.

What will this baby look like? Where is this baby going to sleep? We don't have enough bedrooms for all of us. Does this mean Jerry is staying with us forever? Why can't my daddy be the father?

This was puzzling, but at the same time I was excited to feel the baby in Mom's belly, and she seemed content, though nervous, most of the time. Now I knew why Mom hadn't been going out and drinking since we'd moved here. Maybe this was also the reason she was so concerned with keeping the apartment spotless. She wanted to keep it clean for the baby.

She would let me feel it kick, and it scared me because it looked like a snake dragging across her belly.

"That's the foot. Isn't it neat?" She grinned as the long vine-like thing slithered inside her.

I wasn't sure if I liked seeing it or not, but I liked this nice mom who was comforting.

She took up knitting again, like at the old house. She was making booties and a hat for the baby. She brought me a pair of needles and yarn and showed me how to start the first row. I sat with her at night for hours while we clicked our needles. I was knitting a multicolored scarf because that was simple.

Her fingers slipped through each loop, her expression calm. "Look, I'm almost done. When I finish this one, I will make you some booties so your feet will stay warm at night." She smiled down at me.

I wished we could stay in this moment forever.

My brother and I were playing outside after school, when I saw the car slowly drive up the long, steep driveway, and I knew instantly.

"Dad!" I shouted with joy. Then my ponytail was tugged so hard, I screamed.

My mother was behind me in a hot minute, pulling me by my hair into the apartment.

"Brian, get inside the house now!" Panic swept over her face as my brother ran inside.

I couldn't believe I wasn't able to run to the car and jump into my dad's arms. I missed him so much, I thought my heart would break in two. I heard the car door slam, his feet stamping across the pebbles leading up to our door.

"Pat, I saw you! You can't hide from me anymore," Dad yelled.

He pounded so hard on the door, I thought he would break it down.

My mother placed her hand over her mouth, pointing at us to shush. She crouched away from our front kitchen window so he couldn't see us. We stayed behind her. I wanted Mom to open the door. I wanted to yell out for him to take us.

"Pat, I've been looking for you guys for three months. I need to see my kids. You can't keep them away from me. I know where you are now. Please open the door. I just want to see my kids!"

I cried with him. I didn't think I could live if he left without me seeing him.

He pounded on the door even harder. "I came home to an empty house. I had to search for you in between my days off. I'm not leaving here without seeing them."

The puzzle pieces fit together in my head. She had taken us without telling my father. I needed to see him. I didn't want him to be mad at me for leaving without saying goodbye.

My mother slowly unlocked the latch and opened the door.

I had never seen that look on my father's face. Half-sad, almost teary, while smiling. I knew in my heart he missed us as much as, if not more than, we missed him. "Dad!" I ran into his arms.

He scooped up both my brother and me and hugged us tight.

"Missed . . . you . . . guys," he stuttered as tears fell from his cheeks.

"I missed you so much! We've been waiting for you to come get us." I pulled him into the apartment. I didn't want him to ever leave again, but he stopped before entering.

He looked up at my mom. She nodded yes, and he reluctantly stepped in. It was then he saw her bulging belly. She recoiled away from him.

"Well, this explains a lot. I don't give a crap what you have decided to do with your life, but don't you ever try to keep my kids from me." Dad glared at her.

They sent us into the living room while they talked some things out. My brother and I sat on the couch looking at each other, half hearing what they were saying and half wondering if we could spend time with our dad.

From that day on, when my father was in town, he picked us up. We could either stay with him for the weekend or spend time with him for the day. It wasn't perfect, but at least I knew he was okay and that he loved us.

We were woken up by Jerry's sister Sheila, who came into our room and told us to pack some clothes. She explained that Mom was going to the hospital to have the baby.

I liked Aunt Sheila—she was funny and nice. We spent time at Jerry's mom's house on the weekends when my dad couldn't visit. Jerry came from a large family that included many siblings, and his family became our second family. His mom's name was Rose, just like my grandmother, so we called her Grandma Rose too. An abundance of barbeque meats, chicken, salads, and vegetables always filled the table, and we didn't have to ask to eat—it was there all the time. Some dishes I had never tried before, like lumpia, pork barbeque, and pancit. A whole table was designated for dessert. I'd stuff my belly until I couldn't eat another bite, as we weren't allowed to eat this much at our home. Here, so many people revolved in and out, it was required to never run out of food.

That night we went to Auntie Sheila's house and put our bags in the bedroom. I wandered into the bathroom and saw her poke her eyeball with her finger.

"What are you doing?" I stared at her face.

She giggled. "I wear contacts. They are like glasses you put in your eyes. I have to take them out at night before bedtime." She pulled a clear hard circle out of her eyeball.

"Oh . . . gross." I scrunched my face up.

We laughed, and she hugged me.

"When is Mommy coming home? Do we have to stay here for a long time?" I missed our apartment, even though I liked it here.

"Not too long, honey. I think just overnight, but I'm not sure. We will be going over to Grandma Rose's tomorrow, okay? We can eat breakfast there, and you can play with Auntie Lola."

Yay! I'd be going to Grandma Rose's.

My sister, Kecia, was born and brought home a few days later. She was my little dolly. I loved her the minute I saw her. She had a huge amount of jet-black hair, darker than mine.

"Mom, why is she so hairy! She looks like a little monkey." I cuddled up close to Kecia.

Mom pushed me back a bit. "Don't smother her! All newborns have that. It will fall out over time."

Kecia cried a lot. The diapers were not fun to change or smell, although I loved holding and feeding her. Now three of us slept in the one bedroom. The crib rested against the wall, and my brother and I had our beds side by side. Kecia woke up most nights, which made us too tired to concentrate at school. It made me grumpy, but it was the best having a baby sister.

I thought we would be happy with the new addition to our family, but in a short time, my mother grew restless and started drinking again.

"I can't stay in this cooped-up box of a house all day. I need to get out and breathe." She threw her hands out to her sides dramatically.

She fought with Jerry too. Sometimes he wouldn't come home, which made her anxious. That translated to taking out her frustration on us. Much of that anger was taken out on Brian, since he was the "little man" of the family. He had to go to the store when she was busy with my sister, and that meant buying "women products," which did not make him happy. Mom piled all the manly chores on him. Washing windows, taking out garbage, fixing something in the apartment that should have been done by a repairman.

One time, she grabbed him by the arm and shoved him into the wall. "Why can't you do things right? Are you an idiot? This is a simple repair. Anyone could do it."

To relieve our stress, my brother and I would steal a couple of Jerry's cigarettes and hiked up the hill behind our home to smoke. I think I did more choking than actual smoking, but I felt grown up, tough. It gave me a release from my anxiousness. I loved climbing up to the cool, breezy mountainside. It felt peaceful on a hot summer day.

My mom now walked or rode her bike to the local bars in this new town. One day when riding home, she tried to pedal that bike up the steep hill, and she fell and broke her arm. Our chores stacked up even more because of her injury, and the apartment launched into turmoil. My baby sister and Mom needed more care than I could give, and the caregiving started as soon as I walked through the door after school. We dreaded coming home because Mom would bark orders like a drill sergeant before we even sat down.

"Don't put your stuff here in the kitchen. I've been cooking and taking care of this baby all day. Go take this to your room. Are you guys stupid? Why can't you think for yourselves? You will never amount to anything with this behavior. Get upstairs now! Clean both bathrooms. Take out the trash in all rooms. Fold the clothes on your beds. Make sure you fold them the right way this time."

If we didn't do what she said, she or Jerry beat us. If we did everything she wanted, she still beat us. Everything made her angry.

In between the abuse were snatches of calm, with rosary beads and prayers to a God I feared. My mom prayed fervently over those beads, reciting by rote prayers that were never answered. She would go out on Saturday night and be hungover on Sunday morning. She insisted that Brian and I go to church, though she went only occasionally. It was a short straight walk down a field across from our apartments. We would slide into the back row of the pews and wonder what we were doing there. I made sure I had my doily on my head because Mom said you never entered the church without a covering. Parents looked at us, but no one approached us.

We listened to the priest talk about sins and punishments, which filled me with fear. *Was I a sinner? Does God like me?* I didn't know who I could talk to about my questions. The priest seemed scary.

At one point, my mom insisted my brother become an altar boy, and as soon as we had our Holy Communion, my brother served as an altar boy.

When I attended services one Sunday, the ushers looked around. They were short on people to hand out the baskets to collect the tithe. I had seen it done a dozen times, so I thought I could help. I grabbed a basket from the back of the room. Starting at the back pew, I passed the basket to the man at the end. He gasped and looked at me with his mouth open. He took the basket without taking his eyes off me.

Just then an usher grabbed my arm and hauled me to the front hallway. "You can't pass out the tithe baskets!"

"Why not? You didn't have enough people. I was trying to help you." I stood my ground. My face heated up from embarrassment as he walked away in a huff. I cried and ran to the bathroom. I continually made the wrong choices in this town.

A few weeks later, I waited near the back room of the church for my brother, who was preparing the wine for the next service. I watched from the corner of the hallway, where I was half-hidden. He poured some wine in the decanter.

The priest came up to him and whispered something. My brother shook his head no. The priest slapped him across the face.

I gasped, putting my hand over my mouth so they wouldn't hear me. My brother poured more wine and then walked out. When he saw me, he stopped, then walked right past me and ripped his robe off. He in no uncertain terms told Mom that he would not be an altar boy anymore. By this time, he was taller and stronger than her, and she couldn't make him. She stopped going to church, though Brian and I pretended we still went.

We figured that since she slept in on Sundays, she wouldn't leave the apartment with Kecia and head to church. Every Sunday we'd say we were going to church services, and she would give us each fifty cents for our tithe. We'd promptly walk out the door, but instead of heading straight down the field to church, we would make a hard right toward town.

The donut shop was just about the same distance. When we walked in, the smell of warm donut dough filled our lungs. The glass counters showed us every flavor and style of donut we could purchase. We had just enough money to buy a donut—or two, if we ordered the plain ones and a drink.

I gravitated toward the creamy maple-covered ones with vanilla custard filling. That first bite squished out the center, and it took both my hands to grab it so it didn't fall on the floor. *This is way better than church*, I thought.

We headed back home near the time church was ending. Mom interviewed us upon our return.

"How was church today?"

"Fine."

"What did you learn?"

"Not to sin." I couldn't look directly at her as I lied.

"Okay, well, go play while I rest a little bit more, and then I will make you guys lunch." She rolled over in bed and pulled the covers over her head.

I took my sister and played in the little yard. I was learning to lie with a straight face, but my gut told me it wasn't good.

The fighting started with little disagreements between Jerry and my mom. A meal that was ruined because he came home too late. Something was said that hurt someone's feelings. The yelling escalated to the physical, to the twisting of limbs and punches to the face, to the screams of my mother when the fighting went too far.

Brian and I landed in the middle.

"Stop! Please stop! You're hurting her!" My voice grew hoarse from trying to make Jerry stop.

One evening my brother and I sat on the sofa, in our pajamas. My sister lay cozy next to me in her blanket. We had our TV trays over our thighs, waiting for our chicken soup and buttered saltines. My mom had made this simple dinner because she was getting ready to leave us and go out drinking. We didn't care anymore. If we got dinner and could watch TV while she was gone, it would be calmer because we would finally be alone.

Just as we were slurping our soup, Jerry came home. Slamming the door, he took one look at my mom and lunged at her. As he pushed her back, she fell toward my brother, spilling hot chicken soup all over his lap.

"Aghhhh . . . MOM," screamed my brother as the soup burned through his pajamas to his legs.

It made no difference to them. Jerry pummeled her face with his fists while pushing her legs back and sitting on her. I grabbed my sister and ran out to the patio, jumping the fence to a neighbor's house for protection. My brother followed, crying out in pain, but I had no time to comfort him. We pounded on the neighbor's front door, and she let us in. She had hidden us before. We waited in fear over what was happening at our home, but five minutes later my mom was at the door.

"Kelly, let me in," Mom cried out, desperation in her voice. She limped in, and through the door, we saw that her face was swollen and red.

"Pat, I'm calling the police. I can't hide you guys anymore. These kids are getting hurt. And he needs to be arrested for what he is doing to you," she told my mom.

"Please, no police," Mom said. "I promise I won't let this happen again. I'm going to leave him."

Kelly held us while we sat in a circle on the living room floor. My brother cried. I cried. My mom cried. Kelly brought us tissues and something to drink. She said to relax and breathe.

"You are safe here. Don't cry. I'll protect you." She rubbed my back.

We returned home about fifteen minutes later, after we heard Jerry's car screeching down the street. Jerry didn't come home that night. The next morning, my mom was bruised, and her knee twice its normal size. She couldn't put weight on it, so she made a makeshift cane out of a stick. She took a few steps and fell.

"Mom, we should take you to the doctor." I pleaded with her as her bruised eye turned bluer by the minute.

"No! I'm fine. You can help me with your sister. I'm just going to lay here and get some rest. That's all I need. It will get better . . . I promise." She hobbled to the couch and collapsed.

"I promise it will get better. Someday it won't be like this," she said as if trying to convince herself.

How many times had I heard this promise? That "someday" never came to this apartment. Nothing ever changed.

Jerry stopped coming home after that night.

It took Mom about a week to walk normal again. Our neighbor had a friend who loaned Mom some crutches, and she made her way around better with them, though she slept downstairs on the couch because it was too hard to climb the stairs.

Mom started drinking at the bars again. Some days after school, we would go looking for her when she forgot to leave us a note. She liked two bars the best—the bartenders liked my mom. They knew us and would let us come in for sodas. We'd slide into a booth and wait for Mom. The bars were dark and filled with noise, with music blaring top hits and customers laughing loudly.

One of the bars had shuffleboard, a game I loved. I took the metal disk and slid it across the sand-filled board, hitting the other metal disk and knocking it off to the side.

"Hey, little lady, you are pretty good at this game." A customer patted me on the head.

I smiled back at him proudly. I liked it when someone told me I was good at something.

"Don't you get too close to my daughter," Mom shouted at him. "She's too young for you." She threw her head back and laughed.

My mom was beautiful when she was out at the bars. She wore makeup, with perfect red lips. She combed her hair with a wave falling across her high cheekbones. Her dark-brown eyes had sprinkles of gold in them. She was funnier, lighter, happier.

The problem was, we kids sat in a bar, and we wanted to go home after our soda and shuffleboard, but she wasn't ready. I watched her interact with the men. She tilted her head to the side, her hand on their shoulders or knees. She looked directly at them when she was talking. They were engaged with her words. My mom was magnetic; it was magical to view her in her element.

I tucked away all her tricks, but I didn't like the bars. Old cigar and cigarette smoke filled the air. I liked listening to the music and watching people dance though. I liked the shuffleboard game, but not the hot, drunken breath of people who edged too close or were too handsy.

Lucky for us, we weren't old enough to stay too late. Mom would soon have to walk home with us. A friend watched my sister at our apartment, so Kecia never had to go to the stinky bars.

When we arrived home, Mom took her frustrations out on my brother and me.

"Brian! Get in here right now. I told you to empty this garbage twenty minutes ago," she yelled from the kitchen.

"Mom, I told you to wait. I'm just finishing up my homework," he gruffly answered from the living room.

"This garbage smells. Do it now or else. You make me sick. You never listen. You are worthless," she said as she marched in and stood over him. "I said *now.*" She smacked him across the face.

He narrowed his eyes at her and stood, moving close to her.

She retreated with a panicked look. She had pushed him too far.

He tore out the door, and we followed him. He sprinted into the mountains until we couldn't see him.

Mom looked scared. "Go find your brother and bring him back."

I ran up the mountainside. "Brian, are you there?" Soon tired and hot, I gave up. Why would I want him to come back? He hadn't answered me. Maybe he'd left for good this time. He had done this more frequently these days, fighting my mom back. He wasn't a little boy anymore. He was almost twelve. His fear was turning into rage.

CHAPTER 3

Disneyland Dad

MOST OF THE TIME WHEN Mom took off, she left us in charge of our toddler sister. This made it easier for Mom to go out on dates and stay out late.

When we were with Mom, our days were full of responsibility. When Dad picked us up, he made sure we had fun.

He often took us to his brother's house. Uncle Clarence and Aunt Genny had three boys and three girls, and my favorite cousin was Lynn, who looked like me and was my age.

"Are you two sisters?" asked a lady when we were at the corner store. We giggled. "Yes!" We ran out, laughing.

We felt like sisters, and I wished I could stay with her forever. We walked home, sharing deep, dark secrets.

"What boy do you like at school?"

"Have you kissed anyone?"

"Of all your brothers and sisters, which one is your favorite?"

Our questions came in rapid succession as we chewed on our candy.

Aunt Irene, Dad's sister, joined us at my Uncle Clarence's, as she usually did. The adults sat in this big beautiful house with kids running all around, dogs chasing after them, bunnies in their crates. The adults laughed at us, and we laughed back.

Dinnertime was a drill. With more than twelve people to feed, all the adults helped cook. The smell of barbeque chicken, hot dogs, and hamburgers wafted through the house. When it came time to sit at the table, it was every man for himself. If you didn't grab what you wanted from the meat, potato salad, bread, and all the fixings, you went to bed hungry. We kids ate dessert; the parents poured drinks. We listened to their tales, asked questions, and watched them crack up over stories we didn't understand. Then we played outside before the sky faded to dark.

Bedtime came too soon. We slept with our cousins in their bunkbeds, but sleep eluded us. The hunger in our stomachs never went away. We ran around so much that we were eating machines.

We tiptoed to the kitchen to grab something quick to eat, with a few of her siblings behind us.

"Shhh . . . don't laugh or they'll hear us," Lynn whispered between her giggles.

Try as we might, the adults weren't drunk enough to not notice.

"Get your butts back to bed, you guys! We can hear you!" Aunt Genny stared right at us.

We squealed with laughter and ran back to our rooms. We heard them laughing from the living room, with the clicking of ice against their glasses. This home was filled with love, and my heart was full.

But the weekend flew by too quickly, and Dad drove us back to Mom's apartment.

Mom, not happy to see us, grilled us about what my dad had said about her.

"I know he said something. He always talked bad about me to his brothers and everyone. Just tell me." She towered over us on the couch.

Tears rolled down my cheeks. "Mom, I swear. He was having a good time, and they were telling stories." I didn't want to be in the middle. I loved my mom, I loved my dad, and I didn't want to pick who I loved better.

"You're a liar. You always take your dad's side. You are just like him." She glared at me with disgust.

I couldn't wait until my dad came to get me again.

A few months later Dad showed up to take us on a road trip. He told us we were headed to the snow.

"Daddy, what does the snow feel like? Is it like fluffy clouds? Does it hurt? How long until we get there? Can I play in it when we do?" I was jumping up and down on the seat in the pickup.

"Phylis, sit still. We will be there soon. I found a fun motel to stay at when we get to Reno." Dad smiled big, clearly knowing something we didn't. "Big Blue," our Ford pickup, rolled into town at nighttime. I knew it was Reno because a ginormous bright-red sign announced *RENO*. The sign stretched across the road and arched between the buildings on each side of the street. It was the most vibrant city I had ever seen. Everywhere I looked, bright lights sparkled in the snow.

The cold seeped through the truck. We drove a little past town, to a motel with another lit-up sign: *RIP VAN WINKLE MOTEL.*

"Hey, that's our last name," my brother shouted.

My mouth dropped open. Awestruck, I asked, "Daddy, do you own a motel?"

He laughed loudly. "Um . . . sure."

We walked inside. It was small room with dingy curtains, a bed with an old tattered bedspread in dark-red plaid quilting, and a worn and faded small chair in the corner of the room. A small bathroom held a shower. We shared the bed because Brian and I couldn't sleep by ourselves in another room. I was ten years old, my brother almost twelve. We didn't mind since it was only one night. Tomorrow we would go to a ranch of a friend of my dad's, where we could see their horses.

"So, Daddy, if we own this motel, can we come back whenever we want?" I was already planning the next trip in my head.

"Ha-ha. Sorry, honey. I was just kidding. I don't own the motel. It just has the same last name as ours. I thought it would be fun to stay here."

It didn't matter. We were on an adventure. I didn't have to be an adult this weekend. I would be a kid with no responsibilities.

The next morning, we woke up early and went to a local breakfast joint, where we ate fluffy pancakes, eggs, and ham. We then headed out to Dad's friend's ranch. As we pulled up to their house, I spotted the most beautiful horses.

"Dad, can I ride the horse?" I jumped out of the car.

We met Dad's friends outside, and they gave us a tour of the premises. We finally made it to the gated fence where the horses were kept.

"Phylis, this horse is very gentle, if you want to get on him." The woman held my hand to guide me over.

This shiny, beautiful brown horse stood taller than my whole body. He snorted in my face. I hopped back, then laughed. I touched the side of his face, feeling the smoothness and strength of his cheek. I planted my face to his cheek and hugged him. The woman lifted me on top of him and guided me around the corral, holding a rope. I gripped the majestic creature's mane tight. I had never been on something so big. It was a powerful feeling, sitting atop that horse.

I loved the country—you could have all the animals you wanted on a ranch. I dreamed I'd have five dogs, two cats, a couple of rabbits, two or three horses, chickens, and goats.

When Dad said it was time to go, I gave one more hug to my new horse friend. "I love you. Thank you for letting me ride you," I whispered.

He nodded his head as we laughed at the communication between us.

Next stop for this trip—the snow. As we wound our way up the mountain, I stared in awe at the snow-capped peaks. White powdery blankets cloaked trees whose limbs dripped with icicles, clear daggers ready for war.

When we reached the resort, we hopped right into the snowy- white mantle. It was freezing, and some of it hurt when I fell on it. We threw snowballs, ran around, and made snow angels. When we finished playing, we were starving. Dad took us to a small restaurant, where we gulped down burgers, shakes, fries, and dessert. By the end of the day, exhaustion set in.

This trip would forever be in my memory. The weekends were too short with my father. He was my Disneyland dad, always showing us a good time.

Reality set in as soon as we reached Mom's apartment. It would be months before I'd see Dad again.

My brother couldn't take it anymore. He ran away for good right before his thirteenth birthday. After one more argument with my mom, he'd headed up the hill, never to come back. Mom called my dad later that night, and he said my brother was moving in with him.

My mother, sister, and I were left alone to make it work with no man around. I stayed home alone now with my sister when my mom went out. Most nights I was scared to be by myself, but I made it fun for my sister. We decorated our room together with *Archie* comic book pictures by stapling them to our wooden closet door. We played dolls and had tea parties.

With only one income, Mom couldn't keep up with the bills. My dad gave her money, but most of it was used for alcohol. She complained that my dad never gave her enough.

Our landlord posted an eviction notice to leave by the end of the month. We would have to be strong and creative in figuring out where to go and how to make it affordable.

My mom cried often. "Life is never fair. Don't expect anything from anyone. You will never get what you want. Every time I try, I get kicked in the teeth. You better learn this lesson now." She recited these mantras through her tears.

I worried that we wouldn't have a place to go, that we would end up on the street. I sent up a prayer, asking God to help us right away. Did God really hear prayers from families like ours? I wasn't sure. We had stopped going to church, as I wouldn't go by myself. Not even the donut shop was fun, now that my brother was gone. Was God punishing us because we'd stopped going?

Would we be able to find another place to live? I wondered if God knew I had eaten donuts on Sundays when I should have been praying for our lives. *Was this my fault? Was my mom right? Should I never expect anything good to happen?*

CHAPTER 4

A Baby Grand and Paper Money

DAILY, I SAW PANIC IN my mom's face. It was time to look for a new place to live.

She had met some male friends a few months ago when she'd been at the local bar. Their mom owned a house with a small structure in the back that had once been a garage. It was available if we wanted to rent it.

As soon as we walked in, I loved how cute and spacious it looked. It had a screen door attached to a front door—I could get fresh air on hot days. The narrow hallway to the right led to a big bedroom, and to the left was an L-shaped kitchen that had nice counter space for cooking. A nook to the right was perfect for a kitchen table. The living room was part of this large area, which had another sliding door to the backyard patio area. We could play out there, and it was safe and private. To the right of the living room was a smaller bedroom. My sister and I could share this room. This house seemed perfect for a girl about to start junior high.

My mom, sister, and I moved in the following week. The men who referred us here were nice. I felt calmer than I had been in a long time. Mom seemed happy too, though she struggled to keep a job. Her temper and failure to understand other people's points of view meant she was frequently fired.

A hairdresser by trade, Mom's cosmetology license was her biggest accomplishment. She reminded us often that she could have owned her own beauty shop had we not been born.

I wondered why she thought we were holding her back. I felt like a burden to her.

"If I hadn't had you kids, I could move to Arizona and open my own shop. I know people there. They said I could come down and live there, and I'd be successful. It's just too hard to think about. If I was alone, it would be easier. Holding down a job and trying to get you both ready for school is too much. How am I supposed to keep a job being a single mom?" After her lecture, she somberly looked out the window of our new home.

Except, I always got myself and my sister ready for school in the mornings, and Mom came and went as she pleased.

Why was I here if I wasn't wanted? I didn't want to hold her back from her life. *Why do I have a mom who makes me feel like I'm a hardship for her? Why do I have a dad who is too busy to see me regularly? Why do other kids get to have two parents who dote on them endlessly, when the children take it for granted?*

The trauma and mental abuse haunted me. Mom brought all kinds of people home after a night on the town. It would be the middle of the night. She didn't care. They carried on laughing and drinking. Eventually they passed out, but they would be gone by morning. Before my sister woke up, I picked up the leftover cigarette butts, glasses, and clothing left behind. I didn't want to worry her or have her ask too many questions.

At a new friend's house, I noted how different my world was from Sara's. She lived in a beautiful home. A shiny black baby grand piano sat in her front living room. I fell in love at first sight of that wonderful instrument. I pictured myself sitting on the bench in a sleek new dress with a poufy underskirt. I would put my sparkly shoe on one of the pedals and place my hands gently on the black and white keys. The chords would vibrate through my fingers as soulful music came from my fingertips.

"I wish I could play the piano. You're so lucky to have one," I told Sara wistfully.

"Oh geez! I hate that thing. My mom makes me take lessons after school every Tuesday. I wish I didn't have to." She wrinkled her nose toward the piano.

"I'll fill in for you," I volunteered as I sat on the baby grand's bench.

She laughed, but didn't know I was serious. I would trade lives with her in a second. She didn't know that when I went home, there was no piano, no friendly greeting.

Sara and I went into her kitchen for a snack. Just then her father came home. I flinched, my body tightening up, when I heard the door close. He strode straight into the kitchen. I held my breath as I waited for him to say something mean to us. He planted a big kiss on his wife's lips. That surprised me.

"Hi, girls!" he said. "What are you up too? Did you have a nice day?" His smile was warm and genuine.

As he listened to his daughter tell him about her day, I thought about how fun it would be to share my day with my dad. I missed him. We were on a good schedule now that he had found a job in his town and wasn't traveling anymore. I saw him most weekends, when he wasn't too busy, but it wasn't enough.

I finished my snack and told my friend I had to head home. As I skipped away from the house with the big beautiful piano and loving parents, I dreamed about a day when I would have all the warmth that embodied my friend's home.

At my house, Mom had financial issues. She shared her stress with me.

"Your stupid father has not paid me. How am I supposed to pay the bills? We are lucky we have dinner tonight." She banged the pan on the stove and pulled out a can of Spam and some rice. She slammed utensils around in the kitchen while telling me how disgusting my dad was.

"This weekend when you see him, you better tell him to give you some money. After all, it's your mouth I have to feed."

"Mom, I don't want to ask him. I'm embarrassed to ask him. You do it."

"Don't you tell me what to do, little miss! This is half your fault. If I didn't have to support you, I could have a whole lot more. How do you think you are going to keep living here—with your good looks?" She pushed me out of the way.

I opened the refrigerator. There was a carton of eggs, milk, some seasonings, but not much else. The cupboards were not much better. We needed more money for food.

Soon after that, Mom found a way for us to eat. She applied for welfare and food stamps. Being in the welfare system embarrassed me. Social workers showed up unexpectedly and checked our dresser drawers, piggy banks, and closets to see if we hid money somewhere.

"Do you have any other savings put away somewhere, or any other piggy banks?" The woman filtered through my personal belongings.

I shook my head.

As she made her way through each room, we followed behind to see what exactly she was looking for.

"Some people hide money or other things from us, in their socks, shoes, or different places," she explained as she wrote her report. "You guys look good. Thanks for appeasing me. Sorry, but it's our job." She glanced over at my mom's disapproving expression.

Buying groceries with bills that looked like monopoly money was humiliating. Everyone knew what they were when Mom pulled them out of her wallet. I saw the snide looks from the other mothers waiting in line at the checkout stand.

Our total ran over the amount of approved items, and the cashier blurted, "This isn't covered by your food stamps. You will have to pay cash or put it back." She looked over at the other moms, rolling her eyes.

My mom looked defeated as she shoved some items to the side.

The humiliation chipped away at my confidence. It told me to stay invisible. I stood there next to my mother, watching her face change from mortification to anger. She worked hard, but not hard enough to earn enough of her own money. My mom wouldn't go down without a fight.

She leaned in and glared at this cashier with her steely big brown eyes, pursed her lips tight, and said, "You are the rudest person I've ever met. You are lucky you are behind this counter. If I met you somewhere else, there is no telling what I would do to you."

The cashier took a step back, gulped, and looked back at her register, waiting for my mom to take her groceries and leave. I grinned as we grabbed our groceries. That lady deserved it. At that moment, I was proud of my mom's spunk. I had this same trait—I must have gotten it from her.

This was our life—Mom working at a beauty shop part time and collecting welfare checks to subsidize the rest. She also worked odd jobs when she could.

One of her jobs was washing dishes at a local restaurant. Kecia and I went to meet her there to pick up extra food for our dinner. When we walked in, I heard Mom arguing with some workers. I could see her through the partially open door.

"I'm going as fast as I can." She wiped another dish and put it in the dryer bin.

"Not fast enough," the worker huffed. "You go faster. We want to go home!"

No one could leave until the kitchen was clean. I wanted to get home too. I had homework, and I was tired.

As I entered the kitchen, some of the men said hello in their broken English. I smiled and nodded. They led my sister and me to a table in the empty dining room and brought us some food. I ate my dinner quickly and then told my sister to wait there so I could help Mom.

I entered the kitchen again and sensed my mother's tension. It was exhausting feeling what she felt, but I couldn't help it. I wanted to save her.

"Mom, let me help." I came beside her.

She cried quietly while soaking the dishes and stacking them in the rack. I gently placed my hand on her arm. She was depleted and worn down. She responded well to my approach.

"Thanks, honey. You can dry these and then stack them over there. I'm doing the best I can." She smiled weakly and wiped her tears.

I grabbed a towel and dried with breakneck speed. A worker came in and said I wasn't supposed to be in the kitchen. I lifted my arms up in an I-don't-know-what-to-do gesture and told him I wanted to help. He spoke in Spanish to his coworker, and they shook their heads and left the room. They returned with the manager, who kicked me out. Something about a safety code.

I sat with my sister and sipped my soda. *I could handle this job. Why do I always feel like the grown up?*

Mom finished her shift, and instead of gathering us up and heading home, she wanted to go to the restaurant's bar, which was connected to the restaurant.

"I need a drink to take the edge off this day," she reasoned.

It would be close to 11:00 p.m. by the time we got home. My sister fell asleep while my mom flirted with the men in the bar, and anger flooded me. There were no other kids there. This wasn't normal. But I could do nothing. Once she made up her mind to drink, you didn't mess with her. I waited. Finally, someone offered to drive us home. That would save us the twenty-minute walk to our cottage.

Although there wasn't a man in the house to hurt or yell at us anymore, my mom acted restless. Other than my best friend, Sally, I didn't bring friends over, because I never knew what kind of mood Mom would be in. Sally was the only one who knew all about my mom.

Sally and I had been friends since fifth grade. We'd met over a ladybug.

"Do you want to see my ladybug?" I'd been hanging out by myself, waiting for the bell to signal lunch was over.

Sally had walked toward me, stopped, and watched as I let the ladybug land on my hand and crawl up my arm.

"Sure!" She'd scooted down beside me.

Our BFF status started right there. Sally had long black curly hair and a sprinkling of freckles along her cheekbones. Fair skinned and beautiful, she looked like a princess to me.

Sally came from a single-parent home too. Her mom, Carol, was raising four children, and Sally was one of the middle kids. Carol was cool and dressed in miniskirts and smoked cigarettes.

She hung out with us. "What are you crazy kids up to today?" She met us in the kitchen as we made sandwiches to snack on.

"Nothing. We're going to hang out in the backyard before I have to go home." I smiled at her and gazed at her amazing long legs. She was beautiful with her shiny long brown hair that she flipped back when she laughed. Relaxed and hippy-like, she was nothing like my mom, who wore uptight and conservative clothing. The two women had gone out together before, but they were not alike, so no real friendship had formed.

Sally and I took our sandwiches out to the backyard. We sat on the lawn chairs facing the sun so we could get a tan.

"I can't sit out here too long. I'll burn," Sally informed me again.

I had heard this many times. My Portuguese skin just turned darker with the sun, but Sally ended up looking like a red beet.

"What are you doing this summer?" She rubbed suntan lotion on her arms. "Are you staying here or going to your dad's for the summer? I mean, I know you have that boyfriend there, so you probably don't want to stay here. Will your mom let you go for that long?" Her questions were more for her to find out if we would hang out together.

"I think I'm going to try to stay with my dad. It's just easier there. He doesn't question everything I'm doing. I don't have to worry about taking care of anyone. I don't want to leave my sister for too long though." The guilt of leaving Kecia for the summer weighed heavy on me.

Some days Sally would come by my house, and Mom was cooking and she was happy. On those days we enjoyed fresh-baked cookies with a big glass of milk before doing our chores and homework. Other days Kecia, Sally, and I walked home from school and entered a house full of chaos. I shooed Sally away so I wouldn't be embarrassed.

During one chaotic day, Mom cleaned every nook and cranny. She had our dresser drawers open, with our clothes piled on the floor. The bed sheets and covers were off the bed.

"Everything needs to be redone! It's a mess. It's all unorganized. I want you to refold everything and make the beds over again. When you're done with that, we are going to scrub the bathroom and the baseboards. Now hurry up! I can't believe how worthless you two are. Everything is wrong. You can't ever do things right." She bustled around the house, shaking cleanser everywhere while scrubbing counters as if they had been filthy for years.

The house smelled like powder cleaning solution. It almost choked us. When Mom was manic like this, we knew to stay as quiet as possible. If we did what she said, we could avoid physical abuse.

She scrubbed the baseboards violently with a toothbrush.

We didn't know what we had done wrong. Her mood swings were getting worse. My sister cried as we recleaned our room. I hugged her, trying to comfort her. This was supposed to be my mom's job, comforting a heartbroken child. Except my mother was the offender. I took over as caregiver. My sister was sensitive and sweet in nature, and this was harder for her.

"Just do everything Mom tells you. I will be right here helping too. Don't worry. We can get this all done in no time." I wiped her tears.

She smiled and nodded. We folded our clothes ever so neatly back into their drawers, remaking the beds with the sheets wrapped in tight corners around the edges, just as my mom liked.

Mom was never truly happy. Something was missing. Her moods were very high or very low. There was no in between. She either felt unstoppable in life, or her life was garbage. We couldn't count on or trust her. She promised us the best on good days, only to let us down and inform us that the world was unfair.

She prayed over her rosary beads for a miracle to a God who never came. It never occurred to her to change her behavior. She started her mornings by reading her horoscope. She believed that something in the paper could determine her future.

Then she'd exclaim, "Girls, I have an interview for a new job! This is our new beginning. Just wait and see. Things will get better now. I prayed Hail Mary this morning, and it said in my horoscope that it's my lucky day for good things to happen. I just know it's going to turn around for us." She was giddy with hope.

By late afternoon the tide would change. She didn't get the job. Now she was sure the world, God, the stars, and the moon were against her.

"I try and try. What more should I do? I'm so much better than those young dummies they hire. You'll see. They will call me when those idiots can't handle the job. Where is God now? Doesn't he hear me? What's the use of praying?" She tromped out of the room.

I was now entering high school, and I began to process with reasoning skills. Mom's reactions to life didn't equal the way I responded to struggles. She was my mother. I must respect the way she did things—for now. Somewhere between Mom feeling independent and wishing for someone to take care of her, was loneliness. Deep down I believed that she wanted to be taken care of, to feel safe, and to be loved. I wanted that dream for her, but her way of making that dream a reality was twisted.

She thought she would find her Prince Charming in a bar. He would be sitting on his barstool waiting for her to appear. He would sweep her off her feet and forever take care of us. Even if Prince Charming didn't show up, she must get away from us and the stress from her jobs.

Sometimes she didn't come home after work. I would wait to make dinner, hoping she'd show up and make it for us. Our growling stomachs would win out, and we made dinner for ourselves.

Kecia and I fell into a mother-child relationship. Being eight years younger than me, she looked to me as the parent. I didn't want that role, and it drove a wedge between us. I pushed her away when I felt she was being too clingy.

"Sissy, can you help me with my homework?" Kecia looked up at me from the table.

"Do it yourself! I'm already cooking dinner. I'm not your mother," I replied, irritated by her whining.

I did love her with all my heart, but I was so confused. There was no room for our sisterhood to grow. I was too busy acting like a parent. I just wanted to go out on a Friday night like other kids my age.

CHAPTER 5

Smells like Teen Angst

I WAS BECOMING A GIRL stuck in a mom role I didn't ask for.

Most times when Mom hung out in bars in the evenings, it was a release for her and a relief for Kecia and me. We didn't have to deal with her mood swings.

One night I drifted off to a deep sleep, only to be jolted awake by the front door unlocking, screen door slamming, and sounds of drunken laughter. The kind of laugh where you half laughed, half shrieked. Mom was clearly not alone. I heard a deep voice. A man was with her.

She stumbled straight for our bedroom, flung open the door, and flicked the lights on.

"There they are. My gorgeous daughters. Just like I told you. Girls, wake up and say hello . . ." She moved toward our bed and shook us.

I always pretended to sleep through this part. It had happened many times before. I just let her rattle on, bragging about us to a stranger. Showing us off like the animals at the zoo.

"Look how pretty they are. Doesn't she have pretty hair? You should see them when they are awake more fully."

Funny, she never said this stuff to us when we were awake. Or when she was sober. I believed it was hard for my mom to say nice things to us. I cherished these drunken words because it confirmed deep down that she really loved us. I just didn't appreciate them at 2:00 a.m.

I kept my eyes closed to avoid being forced into the conversation. I just wanted them out of my room. My sister slept through it all. At least, I thought she did. The man didn't seem impressed with us and talked my mom into going to the living room. Mom turned the lights off and shut the door. I took a deep breath. Now I could go back to sleep. In the morning I'd pick up whatever mess she left in the living room.

The conversation on the other side of my door gave me pause though. The man spoke aggressively to my mom. She was having none of it.

"Nooo . . . stoppp it. I'm going to bed." She sounded drunker than usual. "You can do whaateevver you want."

I heard her stagger then slam into the wall before closing her bedroom door.

I figured he would pass out on the couch or go home. He would probably be gone by morning.

When the door to my room opened quietly, my heart stopped. *Why was he coming in here?* I braced myself. I felt cold, my heart pounding up by my throat. He walked to my side of the bed.

"Are you awake?" His drunken breath scorched my neck. He slipped his hand on my shoulder, rubbing down my arm.

"Don't touch me!" I pushed his hand away hard and sat straight up. I stared him down, my body shaking, my face burning with fear and anger. I was ready to fight him if necessary.

"I'm going out to get some matches. I'll be right back. Don't lock the door, okay?"

Those last words came out in my head completely different. I heard it back in a whisper: *Lock the door!*

I nodded, but I knew instinctively what I would do. Something inside me switched. My gut told me what to do next. Or maybe it was my soul. I couldn't tell.

I waited for the man to close the front door. I wanted to stop and cry, but there was no time. I couldn't even feel my feet inch across the floor. I felt like I was flying low on the ground at ten miles per hour. I reached the front door and locked it. Then for good measure, I locked the screen door too. I crawled to my mom's room. She would know what to do. I shook her shoulder.

"Mom . . . please . . . wake up," I whimpered.

She was dead weight. Breathing heavy, she let out a slow moan and kept sleeping. What was wrong with her?

I am on my own.

I started to pray. I was already on my knees. I didn't know what else to do. I asked God to secure every window in the house. They were never locked. Half the time we left them open for fresh air.

I prayed for protection against this madman now banging on the door, demanding to be let in. He tried the handle over and over. He was not giving up. My heart pounded in my ears each time he tried. I felt faint. He rattled the screen door and then headed over to the window in my mom's room. I could see his shadow as I squished down lower by my mom's bed. He pushed the window frame, but it was locked. He proceeded to the other windows. They were all locked. I said a quiet "thank you" to God, who I hoped heard my prayer.

The man cussed and talked to himself as he crunched gravel while walking back to his car. He slammed the door and drove off.

I had won. I was sweating, shaking, petrified. *What if he comes back? He could break a window or force his way in.* I left my mom's room and booked it to our couch, grabbed a blanket on the way. I must stand watch all night. I wasn't scared only for me—I wanted to protect my baby sister. If that man hurt her, I would never forgive myself.

I curled up my legs to my chest and wrapped my arms around my knees. "God, I don't know if that was you, but thank you for helping tonight. Please keep us safe. It's just me. My mom can't help. Guard our house." Tears flowed down my cheeks as I prayed. I hoped He heard me.

As I sat in that cold dark living room, I kept thinking I couldn't do this much longer. I didn't want to be an adult. I was a kid. I should be having fun. I should be hanging out at football games on a Friday night, not fending off strangers in my home. I should feel safe.

The next morning, I woke to find my mom in the kitchen making breakfast.

"Mom, what happened to you last night?" I crossed my arms in defiance.

"What are you talking about? And calm down, young lady. Don't talk to me in that tone of voice," she responded.

I recounted the events of the night before. How she couldn't wake up. Everything that happened with that man.

She looked at me as if I were crazy. "You are so dramatic, Phylis. I'm sure it didn't happen like that. He was a perfectly nice guy. I don't remember you coming into my room. I would have woken up. Just settle down. I need coffee." She turned her back to me and went on cooking breakfast.

But she knew. She knew how drunk she had been—I could see it in her body language. She couldn't look at me. She just wanted to be right so she wouldn't look like a bad mom—again.

My rage came out of nowhere. I grabbed a casserole bowl and threw it across the kitchen. It splashed food with shattered bits of ceramic across the kitchen sink.

My mom's face filled with shock and fear. "Are you losing your mind?"

"I'm sick of you calling me a liar! I won't let you do this anymore. I almost got hurt last night. You don't know this man. He's a stranger.

How do you know he's nice? Because you met him in a bar, and he bought you a drink? I'm done with all of this. I'm leaving." I got in her face and didn't back down.

"Sit down. Relax. Okay, I hear you. Something is wrong with you. If you don't calm down, I'm calling an ambulance. You are not right." My mom looked scared.

I never lost my temper like this. My breathing was staggered. *I can't take it anymore.*

I was fifteen years old. I wanted to be a teenager, not a mom to both my mom and my sister. I was losing my mind. I needed an escape plan.

I sat with my friend Lyla in her bedroom, cross-legged on her bed, a bag of chips between us.

"I need to get away. I can't stand living there anymore." I crunched on a chip.

"Man, I totally know what you mean. I'm the youngest in my family, and I can't do anything because my older sisters tell my parents all the bad things that could happen. I hate them." She took a swig of her soda.

We talked about moving away. We needed a plan, and fantasized about how cool it would be to start over in sunny Southern California.

"We could hitchhike down there. Some kids I know did it. We could go to Los Angeles and get jobs!" Lyla rationalized. "We could get an apartment together and start over. No parents telling us what to do. We are almost grown-ups anyway."

I considered the details. New life, new jobs. Freedom. It sounded romantic.

"Yep, it sounds good, but . . . I don't know." I scratched at her bedspread, pondering our future. As much as I'd love to leave, I was afraid of what might be out there in the world.

"Let me think about it." Then I organized my thoughts out loud. "We will have to start planning it. We will need to pack some clothes, food, stuff like that. Who knows how long we will be on the road before we get there? And money . . . we need enough money to save up to live on once we are there."

There was another reason I hesitated. I had a boyfriend, Scott.

During my next visit to my dad's, Scott said, "You are so gorgeous. Come here." He pulled me closer to him and wrapped his arms around my waist.

I let him kiss me. Scott was sweet. His long blond hair grazed my cheek, and his lips were smooth to touch. We sat at his house smoking pot. I loved hanging out with him, though I didn't care for the pot. My feet tingled, my head fogged, and I was starving.

"I need something to eat. What's in the fridge?" I climbed out of his lap and meandered into the kitchen. I made salami sandwiches and found some corn chips, green onion dip, and a soda.

"Dude! You are hungry!" Scott lay on the couch, laughing at me as I spread out all the food on the coffee table. He reached down, scooped the dip with his corn chip, and moaned with satisfaction.

"So good . . . Babe, grab me a soda too." He took another pull of his joint, then lay back down, blowing out puffs of smoke while coughing.

I tried to think of how to bring up the plan I had talked with Lyla about. Maybe I'd keep it to myself for now, as we hadn't finalized anything yet. It might not happen.

Scott caught me drifting off in thought.

"What's going on?" He stroked my hair and lifted my chin.

"I just hate living with my mom. I wish I could live with my dad. Then I could see you more often. My dad said no for now. He doesn't want people to talk about him raising a girl by himself."

"Ah man, I wish that too, babe. Do you think you can talk him into it?" He scooted closer and hugged me.

I didn't tell him I had an alternate plan in the works.

Mom had promised to let me try out for letter girl at school. It was different than being a cheerleader, but I would still get to go to all the games, wear a uniform, and do some cheers.

"You promise? I mean it, Mom." I tried to read her honesty through her eyes.

"I said yes, didn't I? I know you have been stressed lately. That's probably why you have been acting so weird." She kept wiping the countertops, diverting my stare.

"Mom! I can't try out with the girls and then let them down. Please don't lie to me and promise me something you are going to take back."

"I saved the money you need for the tryout and to buy the uniform. Just have the girls over and practice. I'm serious this time. I promise. I want to be different for you. I will be home for your sister on the nights of the games." She looked pleased with herself.

Inside, I excitedly jumped up and down. I knew better than to show too much emotion in front of her. She might use it later to say I was pressuring her.

The next day I told the girls at school my plan. "We can practice at my house. It will be so fun! You guys have done this before, so you need to show me what I need to do for tryouts." I beamed inside.

My friends promised to show me the ropes and get me on the team.

We practiced our cheers outside for weeks and talked about how fun it would be to stand in the back benches cheering on the Acorns. Just before tryouts, I had memorized almost the whole routine, and I felt like a normal teen for the first time.

My mom viewed me from where she stood in the kitchen and motioned for me to come in.

"Phylis, I hate to do this to you . . ." She flicked her gaze away.

I won't have it. "Don't you dare say it." I gripped the kitchen counter.

"Listen, things in life change. I thought I could handle you doing this. I'm working some night shifts, and someone needs to watch your sister. This is how life works. Don't make a scene." She glanced over at the girls watching us.

"I will never forgive you for this." I stomped out of the room and outside. "Guys, I'm so sorry. We can't practice anymore. I'm not going to be able to try out. My mom has to work nights." I held back tears, but they knew.

I accepted hugs from them then they awkwardly bolted away from my home. I didn't want their pity, but it was what I saw on their faces as they said goodbye. I stormed to my room without saying a word. I wouldn't give Mom the satisfaction of seeing me sad.

I'd put up with it all—nights alone taking care of my sister, wearing hand-me-down clothes because Mom said we couldn't afford new ones, and cooking, cleaning, all of it. I only had a few years left of my high school memories. I was a nobody walking through the school halls. I was invisible to the giggling, happy faces of kids who were allowed to try out for sports, plays, choir, debate team. I didn't know the feeling of having a proud parent sitting in the stands and watching with joy as their child excelled in their talent. I'd given up. I hung with the kids who were like me. We sat on the front steps of the school, smoking cigarettes while watching the good kids walking through the parking lot, heading to class. We piled in cars and headed to the lake to drink and smoke the school day away.

Summer was coming. I talked to Lyla again about running away.

"Maybe we can do it next week. I'm sick of being here. I'm ready to start over." I braided my hair in a long ponytail. I hadn't told Sally. She would probably talk me out of it. She wasn't as unhappy with her home life as I was. Even though she was my best friend, this was one thing we didn't have in common.

"Yes, let's do it. I'm so ready." Lyla high-fived me.

On the morning we'd planned to embark on our journey, Mom was at work and Kecia was home. I lied and told her I was going down the street to Lyla's and I'd be right back.

She knew something was up. "Why do you have a big backpack? Where are you going?" She looked frightened.

My heart sank. I was becoming a liar. "Don't worry. I'll be back soon. Just remember—don't open the door to strangers while I'm gone, okay?" I gave her one last squeeze. She was so innocent and beautiful. She was my little dolly. I turned and walked out the door before I could change my mind.

The day was hotter than usual. We sweat buckets as we stood along the highway in our bell-bottom jeans and cropped T-shirts. Thumbs out, we elicited some honks. Others drove by, but before long, a pickup stopped.

"Hey, where you guys going?" The man looked us over.

"We're heading to Los Angeles. But if you can take us as far as Gilroy, that would be good." I wanted to say goodbye to my dad.

"Hop in the back. I can take you there." He pointed to the bed of the truck.

The truck bed was a sweltering-hot frying pan, and the sun beat on my back through my T-shirt. As the elusive driver sped down the highway, I grabbed hold of the sides, my hands burning, but I didn't want to slide down to the end of the truck and fall out. This was not the glamorous, exciting start I'd thought it would be, yet I was secretly happy we were stopping by my dad's first.

We pulled up to Dad's house, and he came outside to see who was in his driveway.

"What are you doing here?" He looked stunned.

"Dad, Lyla and I are running away. I can't take it anymore. We are going to Los Angeles. I just wanted to come say goodbye," I answered matter of factly.

He glanced at me and then Lyla, who now looked embarrassed. He shook his head.

"Well, it's hot today. You girls thirsty? You might as well come in and get something to snack on and to drink before you head out." He strode ahead of us into the house.

We sat down at the kitchen table, relieved we didn't have to be outside anymore. I had tan lines and red burns on my shoulders from the heat beating on us in the truck. Dad set some sodas and chips on the table and left us alone.

"Is he mad at us? He's so quiet," Lyla whispered.

"I don't think so. I dunno. That's my dad. He doesn't really say much or show a lot of emotion. It's hard to tell. I think he agrees with me though. He knows how my mom is. Maybe he'll give us some money before we go," I said, convinced Dad was on my side.

He reentered the kitchen, sat down, and calmly stated, "I called your mom, Phylis. Lyla, your parents are there too. They figured out you guys ran away. Kecia told them about the backpack, and they saw your missing clothes." He half smiled at our foolishness.

"Honey, did you really think I was going to let you hitchhike to Los Angeles? You need to talk to your mom. I am going to talk to her too. Some things need to change. But you can't run away. They are on the way here to get you." He patted my knee.

Secretly somewhat relieved, I was also petrified. How would my mom react? I didn't really want to go to Los Angeles. I was over it as soon as we were in the hot sun in the back of the truck. I couldn't have handled five more hours like that.

But things needed to change at home. Mom couldn't push me around anymore. I was growing up. I was not her puppet. I would stand my ground and tell her that.

An hour later, a car pulled up, with Lyla's dad driving and the moms as passengers. My dad met my mom out front and stopped her before she stomped into the house. They exchanged words, and Mom nodded.

She entered the kitchen, her demeanor calm and steady. "We are not going to talk about this now. We will have a discussion when you get home, but I'm very happy your dad called and you guys are safe." Mom placed her hand on my shoulder as she directed me to the car.

Lyla's parents seemed upset. There would be no discussion together. Lyla and I gave each other looks that were half questions. *What is going to happen to us?* We drove home in silence.

As soon as we stepped in the front door, my sister apologized. "I'm sorry, Sissy! I got scared. I knew something was happening. Don't be mad at me." She hugged my waist for dear life.

"It's cool. I'm glad I'm home. I need to talk to Mom though, okay?" I pulled away.

Kecia pattered to her room, looking back at me and then closing the bedroom door.

"Well, do you want to tell me what's going on?" Mom motioned for me to sit on the couch with her.

I sat next to her. I spilled my guts about everything. "Mom, I'm not going to live like this anymore. I'm serious. Aside from not being able to do anything like a normal teenager, I can't handle the drinking. You must promise you will stop. It's becoming crazy with you bringing home people every week. I can't handle it. I am not Kecia's mom. You should be home taking care of her, not me. I need to be out more with my friends." The list went on and on as I revealed every emotion.

When I finished, my mom looked me in the eye. I had never seen her so serious. "Phylis, I'm sorry. I don't want to ever have you leave again. Things are going to change around her. I am going to stop going out. You need to be with your friends. But you must help me too. I can't do this alone." She held my hand.

I was not used to this mom. I felt like all my dreams would come true. Then I paused. *Is this a trick? Can I trust her?* Cautiously optimistic, I held out hope.

We went shopping the next day, and she bought me brand-new jeans. I noted her stress when she handed the cashier her money. I almost felt as if I had been manipulative. It took me running away for her to be nice to me. Her words were now guarded and calm. It didn't feel natural or normal. We communicated, not with truth, but with copacetic conversation to avoid ruffled feathers.

The phone call informing us that Grandma Rose from Merced had passed away devastated me. I couldn't imagine never seeing her again. I loved my grandmother more than I realized, and I would miss her thick accent and bear hugs.

Mom, Brian, Kecia, and I made the long drive to attend the funeral with all her relatives. So many tears. I watched my mom's tortured face. She was trying to be strong, but I knew she missed her mother. They'd had a difficult relationship, but with love and laughter in between the pain.

I had discovered through conversations leaking out that my mom had been taken away from Grandma Rose at nine years old. My grandfather had had people lie in court and say his wife was unstable and an alcoholic. Mom and her two brothers had gone to live with their dad, and my mom had become the mother in the family. She'd been abused daily. Mom had told me stories about her father.

Other people had said my mom was sweet and nice when she was a teen, but my grandfather was mean. He chased friends out of the house when she brought them home. I suspected that was why it was difficult for my mom to feel close to my grandmother. She was probably angry that her mother had left her with him and hadn't fought for her.

As we approached my uncles and my cousins, we said our condolences to each other and found our seats. The service was long but beautiful, with lots of white, yellow, and red roses. Many people from town paid their respects. My grandmother had been very loved.

The service ended, and we all journeyed back to Grandma's house to visit. As we pulled up to the house, some men I didn't recognize stood on the sidewalk. Uncle Buzz, who'd left the service early, was talking to the men as they all strode into the house. I slipped out of the car with my brother, sister, and mom. We walked through the kitchen and entered the living room to find my uncle telling the men which things to load into their trucks.

Mom flipped out. "What do you think you're doing? Don't you dare start stealing things from this house. It has to be divided up between all of us siblings—you know that!" She plunked her hands onto her hips.

He laughed at her. "What are you going to do about it? Nothing, that's what. I will take what I please. You got a problem with this, brother?" He speared a look at Uncle Henry, who shook his head.

Always the peacekeeper of the family, Uncle Henry was the sweetest man and would never cause a scene. Uncle Buzz knew this. He forgot, though, that my mom was not about to back down. Neither would I. As he loaded hope chests into the trucks, I heard Grandma's words,

"You promise? One chest for each girl. No forget."

I crossed my arms and cupped my elbows. "Uncle Buzz! One of those chests is mine. The other two are for Uncle Henry's girls, and the last two are for your daughters. Grandma told me."

"Sorry, kid. I can get good money for these. Don't worry. I will keep one for sentimental reasons." He snorted as he kept loading items into his arms.

I wouldn't budge. *I won't leave this house without my chest or without fighting for my other cousins.* I planted myself in front of the truck bed and glared as he tromped out with more furniture to load up. "I'm not leaving until you put that hope chest in our truck, then put the other two in Uncle Henry's truck. I'm not kidding. You are not going to make me go back on Grandma's promise."

"What promise? She didn't say anything. Now who's the liar? You better watch yourself, little lady. You're starting to act like the rest of this family."

He thought he intimidated me. In that moment, I was not scared of him. I was sick of not being heard. There was no "little lady" standing here, just a teen with an attitude.

"You better hear what I'm saying—I would never lie about something like that. Grandma Rose took me in her bedroom one day when I was little and specifically showed me each chest. We had a long conversation about them. I loved her more than anything. Don't you dare turn this into something ugly! You can take anything you want from this house. I am just asking you to respect her wishes and give me this one thing!" Tears streamed, but I focused on his face.

He stared back, tilted his head, squinted his eyes, then shook his head back and forth. "You are just like your mother when she was your age. She never backed down from a fight either." He waved to the men to load up the chest into our truck and then promised to leave the other two in the house until Uncle Henry could get them.

I glanced over at my mom and brother and swore I saw a look of glee and satisfaction on my mom's face I had never seen before. I thought I made her proud of me that day.

I came home from school and knew right away something was wrong. Mom was lying down, and she never did this during the day. She would rather stay busy. If she sat too long, she thought she was being lazy. Lying down wasn't even an option.

"Mom, you okay?" I sat down next to her.

"I really don't feel well. I'll be—"

She started to convulse. Her eyes rolled back, and I only saw the white flickering around her sockets. Her body rocked up and down, and her feet and hands cramped in little twisted, crooked balls. I grabbed her so she wouldn't fall off the couch.

"Mom! What's wrong? Mom . . ."

I wanted to run next door to our landlord for help, but I couldn't leave her. I clutched her fingers, which were now turning into her palms. I tried to straighten them. They were rigid and felt as if they would break if I tried to loosen them. I stayed with her until the shaking subsided. She looked at me with lifeless eyes.

"What . . . happened . . . I . . . oh . . ." She tried to sit up, but I stopped her.

"No. Don't move. You just had a seizure. I'm going to run next door and call an ambulance." I started to rise.

"Stop. No. Just stay here with me for a minute. Let me think. I'm okay. Look, I'm doing better." She gazed down at her twisted fingers. "Rub them! Just rub them. It will get better. Stay here. Give me a minute."

I rubbed her stiffened hands. A few minutes later, they relaxed enough that she could wiggle them.

"See? All better. I think I'm just tired, and my body collapsed. No need to worry."

I was worried. I wondered why she was so afraid of doctors and hospitals. *I don't think my mom is as healthy as I thought.*

Weeks went by, and she stayed home more. There was no other mention of her seizure. Meals were cooked on a regular basis. I helped her in the small kitchen, where we bumped into each other as we maneuvered around. The rhythm of stirring the pots of boiling pasta, mixing the sauce, and pulling warm bread out of the oven was like a dance in unison between us. It was therapy that fed both our souls.

Kecia enjoyed setting the table with pretty glasses and plates and folding paper napkins like they were cloth ones.

Mom was relaxed for the next few weeks, as life transformed to a calmer pattern.

Then the restless behavior reared its ugly head. It started small, with things around the house that seemed to be out of order.

"Why did you put the soap in this drawer? It always goes in the other one. Why can't anything be right in my life." She was making a statement rather than asking.

She broke down one evening while I watched her get more dressed up than usual. "Phylis, I've tried being perfect. I can't take it anymore. I feel like I'm suffocating. You must give me one night. Please? I have been so good staying home with you guys."

She asked me like I was her parent. I didn't know how to respond. If I said no, she would stay home and make our life miserable.

"Just go, Mom. It's fine. I will stay home with Kecia. Just promise me this won't be a weekly thing again." I didn't believe myself even as I was saying it. We both knew that before long, our life would be going back to the way it used to be.

CHAPTER 6

Drugs, Boys, Repeat

"**HOW COULD YOU DO THIS** to me!" Mom's voice shrieked.

"I am not doing this *to you*. I'm doing this *for me*, Mom." I patterned my speech so as not to make her upset.

She had reverted to drinking regularly and staying out late. It had been going on for months now. Summer was approaching, and I was entering my last year of high school.

"What am I going to do without you? Who will watch your sister?" Panic overtook her. She paced through the house in contemplation of a different plan.

In the summer, I would be moving in with my father. He had finally agreed it was time. No little sister to watch. No more adult responsibilities. Mom knew she couldn't make me do anything I didn't want to. She had lost control. Her face faded from anger to surrender.

Dad still lived in Gilroy, the same town where we had once lived as a family. Different home, but the same people we had grown up with. That town had always felt like home. I was excited to get back to my friends and family there.

In my head, I was already decorating the bedroom at my dad's house. I couldn't wait to get out of here. I hadn't had my own room since I was eight years old. I wanted frilly pillows and a fluffy bedspread that I could sit on and listen to my favorite radio station. I needed to de-stress from the past. I looked forward to the freedom of privacy.

The hard part was saying goodbye to my sister. Kecia didn't deserve this. She was my sweet baby sister. I wasn't sure where she could go until she turned eighteen, as her father never came to see her. There was no choice for her, so she had to stay until she was old enough to make her own way.

"Sissy, can I come with you?" Tears welled up as she whispered to me as I packed.

My throat tightened as words worked their way out of my mouth. "I can't take you. I promise to come visit and bring you over as much as I can, okay?" My voice cracked. This was harder than I'd anticipated.

My mother treaded into the room. She used my sister's tears against me. "You are selfish, always wanting your own way! Never thinking of anyone but yourself. Who do you think you are?"

She waved her arm at me as I grabbed clothing out of the closet. "Go ahead and get spoiled by your dad. We'll see how long that lasts. He'll treat you the same way he treated me for years. He doesn't care about you. He's doing this to get back at me." Her words hissed through her teeth.

Her plan didn't work. It did the opposite. She couldn't manipulate me anymore. I hated her right then. Her words cut me deep. I finished throwing clothes in my backpack and thought about never coming back.

"I don't want you to go." Kecia grabbed my waist as I headed to the car.

I knelt at eye level with her. "Listen, I love you. It's time for me to grow up and do other things. I promise I will be back. You can come stay with me and visit." I pulled her away so I could make a fast escape.

I jumped into the car, started the engine, and waved to my mom, who stood by the driveway with her arms crossed. Then I drove away.

I felt free like a prisoner who had done her time and been released. I could dream again.

Summer had started, and I was ready. My first boyfriend, Scott, was long over. I'd had a few others in between, never lasting long. I had long since lost my virginity. Hanging out in a small town with nothing else to do but drive around and get high, you ended up in the backseat of a car on a long dirt road doing things you shouldn't do at midnight. I didn't really have a curfew. My dad, trying to give me freedom, just told me not to stay out all night. He didn't know the first thing about raising a girl. My brother could do whatever he wanted—and I was one step below that. I tried to do the right things, but the people I hung out with didn't support that.

I dated Jack, whom I'd met at the park. I'd thought he was out of my league and hadn't even tried to approach him. He was a muscular, tan, long-blond-hair god. He'd locked eyes with me and walked through the crowd of friends we were with.

"Hey." He stood too close and stared me down.

My knees nearly buckled. I didn't want him to know how I felt. I stared back at him even though I was trembling. "Hey yourself," I stammered back in the coolest way I could, considering I was sweating under my T-shirt.

We started dating right away. I was a magnet for bad boys.

I'd tried dating a nice boy in high school last year. It was romantic and sweet, but as soon as he wanted to meet my mom, I had broken it off. Good boys came from good homes. They wouldn't understand crazy.

Bad boys didn't care. They were much more exciting. Jack drove too fast, drank too much, had great drugs, and loved me fiercely. I felt tingly when he pulled me in for a kiss. I thought I was in love. When he undressed me, I couldn't breathe—but guilt built too.

Jack lived on danger. His father had died in a car accident when Jack was three years old. I sometimes thought Jack had a death wish. It was why he drove so fast down the same hill where his dad had had the accident. Jack loved to accelerate down the mountain, never using the brakes. The wheels screeched as if crying to slow down.

I screamed. "Please slow down! I don't want to die! You're scaring me." I gripped the seat and slid around while pushing my feet into the floorboard.

"Calm down, babe. I got this. Done it a million times. I know this road like the back of my hand."

He spun the wheel around another tight curve as the car tipped to the side. We almost hit the mountain at one point, then we were at the bottom. "There, see? Piece of cake." He laughed in that sexy, gravelly tone.

And just like that, I felt alive. I couldn't lie. I loved the excitement.

He was also the sweetest person when we were alone. He told me he loved me, that he had never felt this way about anyone else before.

"You are so beautiful. Why do you hide behind these?" He pulled off my glasses.

I couldn't see a thing.

"There. Gorgeous. You know you have the most beautiful big brown eyes, don't you?" He stroked my hair and kissed my cheek.

I honestly didn't know. I didn't ever feel beautiful. Not like that.

My mind drifted back to when I'd been in a bathroom at school recently. I'd taken my glasses off to rub something out of my eye.

The mean girl had scrunched her face up at me. "Oh geez! Your eyes are huge! You look like those cartoon fish with the big eyes. Gross."

I had looked in the mirror, threw my glasses back on, shot her a dirty look, and ran out of the bathroom. I was ugly. I would never be pretty like the other girls.

"Hey, where did you go?" Jack held my face in his hands.

"Oh, nowhere. I just . . . I think you're silly. Now give me my glasses." I grabbed them and put them back on right away.

"Phylis, quit hiding behind these. I'm serious. Do you know how beautiful you are?" He held my hands.

I smiled back at him. He wouldn't make something like this up. He was being honest. At home that night, I took a long look in the mirror, without my glasses on. I liked the shape of my face. My high cheekbones and long, thin nose, with a strong jawbone, were good features for this face. I did have big brown eyes. Just like my mother. My body was strong, tan, and thin. I needed to stop being insecure. I looked different because I was.

I am a Portuguese girl. I am not a blond-haired, blue-eyed girl. I am starting to feel comfortable in my skin.

I had always compared my looks to my mom. Could I measure up to her beauty? It was confusing, admiring my mother while at the same time being embarrassed by her. Jack would never meet her. She would say something that would chase him away. I was positive of that. Lucky for me, she never came to visit. Unless I decided to bring Jack to her, he would never know her.

I walked into the living room, where Dad was reading the paper. I sat down on the couch next to him. "Dad, I know what I want for my birthday this year. I want contacts." I smiled to myself as we settled in to watch TV.

Jack and I were having a blast. We hung out every day, traveling to friends' houses that were in the country. That translated to loud music, beer, and all the cocaine we could snort, with no nosy neighbors around. During one visit, someone barbecued chicken and hamburgers while we girls made macaroni salad, garlic bread, beans, and corn. I could have stayed there forever. I swayed to the music as I stirred the beans on the stove. Jack came in with a mirror in his hand and some white fluffy powder lined up in two neat rows.

"Here, babe. Take a hit." He handed me the rolled-up dollar bill.

I took it, scooping both piles right up my nostrils.

We laughed and danced together in the kitchen, without a care in the world.

The next morning, Jack told me to meet him at his house. He let me know when I arrived that we would do a pickup. My boyfriend was a drug dealer. I didn't normally go with him, but for some reason he wanted me to this time. I figured I'd wait in the car until he was done.

Jack asked me to come upstairs to the apartment to make the deal with him. I couldn't explain it, but I was nervous climbing up the steps. He knocked twice and walked right in. Curtains were drawn; the room was dark and musky.

Two men sat on the couch, drugs and paraphernalia strewn about on the dirty, dusty coffee table. Guns rested by their sides. They had their hands on them, until they saw Jack. They glanced over at me with bloodshot, glazed-over eyes. They gave me a quick once-over, shook their heads at Jack, then went back to watching some mindless TV show, puffing on cigarettes and sipping their beers.

You could always feel evil. It didn't lurk in the darkness. It permeated your whole body. It was heavy in the room. A vise clamped my lungs. I was afraid if I gulped, they'd see my fear. Why had Jack brought me up here? He loved living on the edge, and now he was including me.

The dealer entered from a back room. "What the hell is she doing here?" He pointed at me. He was a tall, lanky man with a scruffy black-brown beard and a serious scowl.

Jack laughed.

Is that a defensive laugh? Is he as scared as I am? I can't read the room. Is this a setup? Worst yet, am I being set up? Alarm bells went off in my mind, signaling me to stay calm. I'd thought we were picking up a couple of bags of cocaine. This was something different. Strangers weren't invited to this party.

"She's my girl. Don't worry. She's cool," Jack answered.

"I don't know her. Why did you bring her here?" He walked toward Jack, blocking the hallway.

Am I going to get shot today? Maybe worse than death—there were three strange men here. My mind raced to that awful place where girls got hurt when men took advantage. I put my tough-girl face on. I said nothing. Better to assess the situation. Run if I needed to, or fight like hell to get out and save myself as best I could.

I let the men knock it out verbally. We made it through the hallway and were now in the bedroom. Drug Dealer headed into another room. He walked back in with the biggest bag of cocaine I'd ever seen up close. This, however, was not what caught my eye. It was what was in his other hand that made me curious.

Jack sat on the bed. He put a pillow behind his head and sprawled his legs out straight on top of the dull flowery bedspread. He rolled up his sleeve. I clamped my jaw to keep it from dropping open. He couldn't possibly be doing what I thought he was about to do.

The thing in the drug dealer's hand was a brown leather wrapped-up pouch. As he unwound it, he revealed a syringe, plastic pipe, bent spoon, and rubber tie-off.

I had never seen any of these items except in the movies. My world shifted.

Jack took the rubber tie-off and wrapped it around his arm.

"Babe, what are you doing?' I pleaded with him through my eyes. It was not working.

"Don't worry, babe. I am testing the stuff out. It's fine," he said.

It wasn't fine. He would be high. I would be left here with men who didn't know me or want me here.

"Don't worry. You're next, sweetie," mocked the drug dealer, winking.

Sweat formed on my forehead.

"I don't shoot up." I responded as strongly as my quavering voice would allow. The baby hairs on my upper arms flew up.

He laughed.

I am staring at the devil.

"Today you will," he said, deadpan.

I am strong. I am a truck-driver's daughter. My mom had always taught me to never back down.

"Don't let men push you around," she'd say. Even though she did all the time. Men took advantage of her, beat her, lied to her, cheated on her.

I can handle my life better. But maybe I couldn't.

"I will never shoot up. I will snort some if you want me to, but I won't shoot up." I said it twice for emphasis. Maybe I was trying to convince myself. I looked him straight in the eye with determination and held his gaze.

He stared at me, then glanced at Jack.

Jack's eyes rolled back, and his head hit the pillow. He leaned back and let out a huge sigh as his mouth dropped open.

Drug Dealer looked at him with a triumphant smile. "He's good." Drug Dealer laughed.

The insides of my stomach churned.

His attention was now back at me. "Okay, princess, I'll get some stuff ready for you to snort." He staggered into the next bedroom.

I took a deep breath and focused on Jack. I was disgusted with him. How could he leave me in this mess? *I love him. I'm the mess. I must be. Otherwise, why would I allow myself to get mixed up in all this?* I would stay steady until I could get us out of here safely.

Drug Dealer entered with all the things I needed to get high. I thought I felt God protecting me. That seemed strange, but I was having a silent conversation with him as I was about to get high, begging and praying that I would not be hurt by these strangers. I thanked him in advance for helping me get out of there alive, but I wondered if he listened to someone as disgusting as me.

An hour later we walked out from the dark apartment into bright sunlight. I was so high I could barely feel my face. I gritted my teeth, trying to make it down the stairs without stumbling. I had never snorted cocaine that pure before. It shot straight to my brain, and I hadn't come down since the first hit.

I smacked Jack hard in the arm as soon as I slammed my car door. "Why would you take me in there? And since when did you start shooting up? I've never seen you do that."

My questions were many, but he didn't have a good answer. The damage had already been done. This was my life. He was my boyfriend. I loved him, and my moral compass was being chipped away bit by bit. I made excuses for him because I didn't want to let him go. I'd thought I was strong and in control, but I was wrong. My common sense made no sense. How long could I—would I—adjust my own morals for someone else's?

CHAPTER 7

My Mom Is Homeless, and I'm a Mess

I DROVE TO JACK'S HOUSE to surprise him with a home-cooked meal. He wasn't expecting me. He now lived with a couple of his friends out in the country. I steered up the path, looking at the rows of oak trees. I loved seeing lush greenery. I smelled all the foliage and flowers as I slid out of the car.

I put the bags of food in the kitchen and heard the shower running. I walked down the hallway and heard a girl's voice coming from the bathroom. His sexy laugh came next. I threw the door open, and he moved the shower curtain to the side. Just enough so I could see the top half of his naked body, but carefully keeping it closed so as not to see what lay behind the whole curtain.

"Who's in there with you?" I held back my tears. I knew. She had been coming to all the parties lately. She always hung on him, and he didn't push her away.

"Babe . . . what . . . why are you here?" He jumped out and grabbed a towel to wrap around his waist.

I marched past him and ripped the curtain all the way back. "Get out! Get out of my face. I can't believe this. I swear . . . I'm going to kill you!" I lunged at her.

He grabbed me and told her to get dressed and leave.

She smirked at me and didn't move. I wanted to kick the crap out of her. I was no fighter though. I just wanted her gone. She sauntered out of the room bare naked, like a prized gazelle that we should all gaze at.

"Babe . . . let me explain. She came on to me. You know I love you." Jack was pleading with me.

I didn't want to stay. The thought of him being with someone else was too much for my heart. He'd told me he loved me. He'd said if he ever got married, it would be to me. What did he tell her when they were alone?

I needed some time. I hung out with my friends at different houses now, giving myself time to be alone. A few weeks later, I went to a party. I wore contacts now, and guys noticed me. I wasn't used to all this attention.

I was usually the plain girl with the funny personality. Now I was the cute girl with the funny personality.

One guy, Billy, tried hard to get my attention. Nothing like Jack, Billy was Spanish and Irish, dark skinned, lanky, and macho. He walked with a strut, his chest puffed out. He laughed loud and boisterous. I was attracted to men who seemed like they could protect me.

Over the next few months Jack and Billy fought for me. I played off them, gloating secretly. One month I was with Jack. The next with Billy. Whoever treated me better was the man I would stay with. They both promised me forever, and they both cheated on me.

We all got high. No one thought clearly about our futures. I was finishing up my last year of high school, trying to juggle my classes and boyfriends.

My dad was patient with me, but I could tell he was worried. I raced home from school most days, made a sandwich, licking the last bit of mustard off the knife, shoved the sandwich down my throat, and dashed back out the door, telling Dad I had to meet whichever boyfriend I was with that month. I was finally doing the normal things a teen did. My old life with Mom was gone.

Until it wasn't.

"Phylis? This is Margaret. I'm calling because I don't know what else to do. I can't get ahold of your mom, and Kecia is in the house by herself. I can hear her crying. She won't answer the door. But she said she wants you." She stopped to take a breath. "Can you come get her? I'm afraid your mom won't be home for a while. It's getting dark, and I don't think Kecia should be alone." She knew my sister was afraid of the dark.

"I can't come tonight. My dad has my car. My brother is out. There is no way to get ahold of either of them. I'm sorry. I will try to get her if I can." I sat down on the couch as I hung up the phone.

Mom knew Kecia's fear of the dark. I imagined her terrified as she wandered through each room, waiting for Mom to come home. I hadn't been able to see Kecia as much as I wanted to lately. Guilt mixed in with my concern for her. There was nothing I could do until I had a car.

The next morning the phone rang again.

"Phylis!" Mom screamed. "He took her. Help me! He left a note!"

My pulse beat rapidly. "Mom, calm down. Who took her? What's happening?"

"Her father! He took Kecia. He left a note saying he was taking me to court! He said I will never see her again. He can't do that, right?" she asked, as if I had the answer.

"I don't know. Where were you last night?" Though I already knew the answer. "The landlord called me. She wanted me to come get Kecia."

"Why didn't you come get her? None of this would have happened if you were here." She was now accusing me.

"I'm on my way over so we can figure out what we need to do."

Jerry never came to see Kecia. He'd remarried and had a new family with two daughters. Maybe he just wanted to scare my mom so she would take better care of Kecia.

A half hour later, I walked into Mom's house. She sat on the couch, crying, with the note in her hand. "Why did he do this? He has no right."

She sobbed on the note as I took it out of her hands. It indeed said my sister would never come home again. He was taking Mom to court for unfit mothering.

"I told you this would happen if you didn't stop drinking. You know Kecia is afraid of the dark too. Why didn't you just come home?" I shouted, standing over her.

"I should be able to do whatever I please. Nobody has a right to come in my house and tell me how to live." She was defiant in her defense.

But someone did. And now we would have to figure out how to fix it.

As we awaited a court date, I was called to the principal's office at school. The counselor invited me into her room. I took a seat on one of the chairs opposite her.

"Phylis, we've been looking over your records for graduation. It looks like you are a semester short. You won't be able to walk in graduation with your class. You will also need to take summer classes in order to graduate." She rattled the papers on her desk.

I shuffled my feet and looked away. All those months of cutting school, thinking I was so cool. I'd just screwed myself. I couldn't do this anymore. I didn't want to be in school. I needed to get on with my life. This woman had no idea the stress I was under. I had adult problems to worry about, like how I could get my sister back home to Mom.

"Thanks for letting me know. Let me think about what I'm going to do, and I'll let you know." I avoided her eyes because I knew I would never see her again.

"Okay, but, Phylis, we need to figure this out so you can graduate. Please let me know in the next few days."

That was the last time I sat in that office. I quit school a few days later.

The court date was set for the custody hearing. Mom had secured a public defender. The lawyer went over what my mom should say and when to not say anything. Mom was still trying to defend leaving my sister alone. They hashed out situations that might come up in cross-examinations. The court day arrived, and a friend of my mom's drove us to the courthouse. I couldn't drive her because my dad needed the car, and Mom still hadn't learned to drive.

"There is no way a judge will take a child away from a mother," Mom stated matter of factly. "He can't take care of her. He already has enough children. Why would he want her now? He never came to see her before." With every word, she became more convinced she would win this case.

I slumped in the backseat, not so sure it would go the way she thought. I knew her habits. If Jerry's lawyer called any witnesses to talk about how my mother behaved, the judge might not think she was the best parent to take care of Kecia.

We walked through the double doors of the courthouse. The hallways were expansive and cold. The floors were marble, with dark-brown furniture everywhere. We took an elevator to the third floor. As the doors slid open, I saw my sister sitting on the bench. We locked eyes and ran toward each other.

"Sissy!" Kecia came in for a big hug.

I nodded at her father, but didn't talk to anyone else. I was mainly here for her so she didn't get scared.

"I'm going to be right here with you while the adults go inside, okay?" I gave her a squeeze for reassurance. We watched them file into the courtroom, then we waited on the bench in the hall.

"Am I going to be able to go back home to Mommy?" Kecia looked at me with innocent big brown eyes.

Scared to answer, I said, "Honestly, I don't know. I don't see why not. I mean, most judges want the moms to have custody of the kids." I half convinced myself.

We talked about the new sisters she had met and how she was getting along with her dad and his wife. She seemed healthy enough. I wondered if maybe she was better off with this family. I knew it would destroy my mother if she didn't get Kecia back.

We waited. The doors opened, the parties streaming out one by one. I spotted the look on Mom's face. My heart sank, and I steadied myself.

"Kecia, you have to go with your father. You can't come home with me," Mom coldly told her, as if she were ordering lunch. Clearly in shock, she was pretending this wasn't real.

My sister's mouth dropped open and let out a wail. "No! I want to go home with you. I don't want to go back with him." She twisted away and grabbed me around the neck. "Don't let them take me. Please, Sissy! Can't I go home with you? I'll be good. I promise. Don't make me go." She gripped me for dear life.

I couldn't take it. I sobbed with her. I hated adults. They were so selfish. Angrier than I'd ever been, I said words I shouldn't have said. I knew secrets I shouldn't know. "I can't believe you are doing this! You have never come to see Kecia before. Why do you care now? Mom told me you wanted her to have an abortion. You never even wanted Kecia."

Everyone stopped talking. They all stared at me, shocked. As soon as I said them, I wanted to take the words back. I shouldn't be sharing this in public. My focus needed to be on my sister.

"I promise I will come see you as much as I can. You need to go with your dad. It's going to be okay. I love you so much." I tried to loosen her hands from around my neck.

She wouldn't budge. "No. I want to stay with you. Don't make me go." Her crying worsened.

"Give me a minute with her. Please." I knelt next to Kecia, looking up at them.

They walked away. I didn't know what to do except make her feel safe.

I looked at her face to face. "Look, I don't have a choice in this. But I can promise you that if you go with your dad today, I will come see you this weekend, okay? Then it will only be a few days before I see you again."

She calmed down, and her grip loosened. "You promise?" She wiped her tears.

"Of course! I want to visit as much as I can. It won't be that different than when you were with Mom. I had to come visit you then."

The reasoning seemed to work. We paced to Mom, Jerry, and the lawyers.

"I promised her I would come see her this weekend. That's okay, right?" I stared Jerry down.

"Of course. You can come visit anytime," he reassured, taking Kecia's hand.

As they strode off, Kecia looked back at me, and I heard Mom crying.

This wasn't my life. It was my mother's. So why did I feel like I'd just lost my own child?

Mom was not doing well. I frequently stopped by to check on her, and she was never home. She'd lost her job, and I didn't want to spend my days tracking her down at the bars.

I visited my sister as often as possible. She was doing fine, but a sadness settled in her eyes, so I brought her to my dad's house to spend the night.

My dad welcomed her. "She's a sweet girl. None of this is her fault. She can come over anytime you want her to, or whenever she wants," Dad reassured me.

He understood the mess in all this. Soon I'd be moving out on my own and could take Kecia to my own apartment. I wished she could live with me, but she still needed to go to school. Plus, I was barely getting by with my job at the local Dairy Queen. My girlfriends and I had worked out a plan to share the rent. We could afford it if we split it three ways.

When I finally talked to my mom, she sounded depressed. She didn't ask how I was doing.

She never did.

Her own problems were foremost on her mind, and it couldn't be filled with anything more. "I'm getting kicked out of my house. I can't pay the rent anymore. I need to put my stuff in storage, so a friend of mine has offered to keep everything at his house. Just until I get situated somewhere else."

"Can I come get a few things? I really want my dresser and mirror." I needed it now that I was moving out on my own.

We agreed to a time for me to grab some items. Then she added one more thing before she hung up. "This could have all been different if Kecia was here. I just don't care anymore."

There was truth to that statement. She had been much more despondent since my sister was gone. She'd just given up. I asked her where she would be staying.

"I'm leaving town. I can't take it here anymore. No one will give me a job. I'm moving back to San Jose. I'll let you know when I get settled."

She assured me she had a friend's couch to sleep on. We hung up, and I shook my head. I was moving into my first apartment, and my mom was homeless.

CHAPTER 8

The "A" Word

I MOVED IN WITH MY best friends Sally and Jesse. Since I paid a bit more for rent, I slept in the biggest bedroom. Sally stayed in the second bedroom, and Jesse slept on the couch, since she paid the least.

We were each dating someone. I was, for the moment, back with Billy. All the boyfriends became friends, and soon after a while, they moved in with us. Now six people lived in a two-bedroom apartment. We spent the days working and the nights partying, either with the six of us or with other neighbors and friends. It was not unusual to have the doors open to all the apartments, hamburgers on the barbeque, and loud music blaring out of one of the apartments while we all trekked house to house, beers in one hand, cigarettes in the other. We often ended up on the front lawn, hanging out weekend after weekend, soaking in the warm summer nights.

I would come home from work at the end of the day smelling like burnt onions, hamburger meat, and vanilla milkshakes. I couldn't wait to take a shower and change into clothes that showed off my slim but curvy figure. I used my sexuality every chance I could. The attention I craved had never been given to me as a child, and now I filled it with any man's attention.

I knew I was repeating the same habits I had watched my mom act on years ago. I now understood the power behind it. I felt like the most important person in the room. The reality was, it was a quick high that needed to be repeated over and over.

Billy and I had a tumultuous relationship. Some days were loving and caring. Other days he lied to me. At least, I thought he did. He'd say he was going to see his sister, but then she would show up at my apartment. When he returned home, he had an excuse.

"I did go by to see her, but she wasn't there, so I stopped by the store. Stop being so paranoid. Here. I picked up some beers and chips." He set the bags on the counter.

I felt like an idiot, but I had a funny feeling in my gut. I watched him for any sign in his body language, but he was skilled. He knew I watched him, and he kissed me to throw me off.

"You're cute when you're jealous." He grabbed me and pulled me close.

I was embarrassed because now all the roommates were watching us.

"Stop! You're stupid." I giggled and pushed him away from me. I looked over at his sister sitting on the couch. She averted her eyes, and I swallowed my pride. I knew he was probably lying. I just didn't want to fight in front of everyone.

The next day we were at his parents' house for lunch. His mom, Laura, cooked a feast for the whole family. Saturday brunch was a tradition in her house.

I came in and kissed her cheek. "Hey, Mom. Whatcha making?" I scooped up a tortilla chip with guacamole.

"Hi, sweetie. Just a little of this and that. Do you want to set the table for us?"

I grabbed the plates and started laying them out across the tattered, dinged-up wooden table. This table had served many meals with loud, boisterous people who loved to tell stories while we ate. I liked Billy's family. They were strict but loving, though sometimes the fights were intense between Billy and his father.

I'd seen his father raise a hand to strike Billy before his mom stepped in to calm the situation. Other days they were all kissing and hugging like they couldn't live without each other. I was used to this turbulence; it was much like my own family before my parents split up. I was comfortable with this family dynamic.

Laura told me she wanted her son to marry me. "My Billy adores you. He told me he loves you and will marry you someday. I love you too, Phylis. You are good for him. He is so happy when he is with you. I know he's not perfect, but he will change once you guys are married. Billy's dad used to run around with other women too, but I know he is faithful to me now."

I wasn't comforted by her words. I loved her son, but I knew I didn't want any man cheating on me, especially if I was going to spend my life with him. I gazed outside to the backyard. The lawn was yellowish and patchy in areas. There was half a patio set on the concrete; a few of the chairs were missing, and the rest were worn and rusty. The wooden containers held lifeless, limp flowers hanging over the edge. New growth of grass did grow where Billy's dad had started to till the backyard. They were working on making it better for summer parties.

I related that yard to the messy chaos in my relationship with Billy, but we were working on it.

Apartment life was messy too. There were too many people living in too small a space. We waited for the bathroom to be free, there was no privacy, and food was scarce. When one roommate would buy something, someone else would eat it. Most of the time, food was there for everyone, but I was still a girl on a tight budget.

I made a store run to pick up some food for me to eat for the week. I marked my name on each box and package. I wanted to be sure it would be there at the end of the day. I had bought some pork chops for Billy and me, as I wanted to make us a nice dinner. I was playing house, and salivating while dreaming of that delicious pork chop dinner as I flipped yet another hamburger at work.

After work, I raced home to start preparing everything before Billy arrived. I ran to my bedroom to change clothes and then sauntered into the kitchen. All I saw as I opened the refrigerator door was open space where the pork chops had been. I checked the vegetable bins, the freezer, the shelves behind other items. The pork chops were gone. I stood there with the door open, wishing them to reappear. I started to cry over the missing pork chops.

It wasn't about the food so much, though. I loved living on my own—I just hadn't planned on living with so many people. People who took your things because they thought it was a free-for-all in this house.

I pondered having a mom to check in with, to see if this was the best direction for my life, to be in this crazy situation with so many people. Then I remembered who my mom was. She was always in sticky situations, so her advice would do me no good, even if she was around.

Mom had been sleeping on some man's couch, and the man was in a wheelchair. She helped him and stayed there for free. Not the best accommodations, but the last I talked to her, she'd said it was better than the shelters.

"I'm not staying at the shelter anymore," Mom said. "They stole my wallet and the last of the money I had and my identification. It's not safe there."

There was no asking how I was doing. She didn't have room for that in her life.

"Can you lend me a few dollars?" she asked. "Just until I get a job. I have an interview with a deli market."

"Mom, I can barely afford my rent. I can't right now." She made me feel guilty for the negative response. We small-talked, and she hung up without asking what I needed from her. I felt more frustrated after I talked to her.

Where would I find the strength to figure out my future?

Billy and I fought more than ever. He moved out of the apartment, and I saw signs that he was cheating on me. I heard the rumors, but each time I tried to break up, he surrounded me with tears, flowers, and promises that he loved me more than ever. I wanted to believe him. He had a wonderful family who loved me. They were convinced Billy would marry me someday.

Something in my gut told me it wasn't right, but I told my gut to shut up and stuffed down my intuition screaming at me to run far, far away.

The afternoon started off perfect. Summer was coming to an end, but for now the sun was shining so bright, it led to a lazy day of pool, drinks, and relaxation. I was waiting for Billy at our friend Todd's house, where Billy had told me to meet him. I'd arrived with my swimsuit under my tank top and jean shorts. I loved lying by a pool with drink in hand.

Todd lived in the country, his house surrounded by beautiful green bushes and pink and white hydrangeas. The mountaintops were part of the view in the luscious backyard.

"It's so hot, I'm going to jump in now. Is that okay?" I waited for Todd's permission.

"Of course. Billy should be here soon. Want a beer?"

I jumped in and felt the cool water freeze up against my hot skin. Swishing around, the water regulated to the perfect temperature to swim around in.

As Todd brought my beer, he talked nonstop about silly things that I wasn't interested in. I tried to stay engaged, but I wondered why he was talking so much. It wasn't his normal personality.

A half hour went by. Todd was wandering around, trying to stay busy but not talking anymore.

"Todd, what time did Billy say he was coming?"

"Uh . . . soon, really soon . . . I don't know, really." He rambled on, and I instantly knew why.

"Todd, are you supposed to keep me here? Where is Billy? Is he at his house with someone?"

"Wait. Don't tell him I told you. He will kill me. I hate that I had to do this. You're a nice girl. I'm sorry." He begged me not blow his cover.

I jumped up and threw on my top, wiggled my shorts over my wet bottoms, and jumped into my car. I couldn't believe how stupid I was. Why hadn't I figured this out before? Billy hadn't wanted to pick me up. He'd told me to meet him there.

I raced into town, parked my car in his driveway, and ran to the front door. I banged my close-fisted hand against the door. "I know you are in there with someone. Don't pretend you're not home. I will pound on this door until you open it."

Billy slowly opened the door with a slight grin on his face, as if he would enjoy the attention he was about to get from me.

But I marched past him, past the living room, to the bedroom. "I know you are here. You better come out now!" I yelled.

The bedroom door opened, and there she was—a random girl I didn't even know. I was right. Billy was cheating on me and was likely telling her the same things he told me. It probably wasn't all her fault. She ran past me and out the front door.

I was glad she left. I had no plans to harm her—I just needed proof. "I can't believe you have done this," I screamed, and he pushed me out of the way, to shut me up. I felt a rush of red-colored rage flow through my cheeks and burst through my body. I'd sworn no man would ever touch me the way they had touched my mother.

I slammed him up against the wall. "Don't you *ever* touch me like that again. I will kill you." Panting, I spit out my words. I had my hand up against his chest so tight, he shrank back against the wall.

Todd rushed into the house and pulled me away from Billy. I couldn't do it anymore. I walked out of the house and drove away. I was finished with this relationship forever. We'd crossed a line that would have continued to a violent end.

I stayed strong in my resolve to avoid Billy. Months went by. I went to a party, and there he was, staring at me in that way he did. I tried to avoid him by talking to my friend Lisa Grass.

She was recently engaged and told me she was moving to San Jose to start a new life. "Rick and I need to get it together and stop partying so much. We are going to have a baby." She rubbed her belly as proof.

"What? That's cool! So that's why you're not drinking tonight?" I was proud of her, and a bit jealous.

At the end of the night, Billy offered me a ride home. I had come with some girlfriends, so I told them he would drive me home—they didn't approve, but didn't try to talk me out of it. Billy and I ended up on a dark side street, and I gave in to him one last time. *It's just one night. I won't go back to him.*

And I didn't.

Soon after, the apartment sharing didn't work out anymore, and I moved back home with my dad. Though we roommates went our separate ways, we saw each other often. I was unemployed and taking typing classes at night at the local college. If I could improve that, I could get an office job.

But I was not feeling well. Nauseous and dizzy, I thought I had the worst flu of my life. Then I checked the calendar and went to a clinic for a blood test.

I was two months pregnant.

"What am I going to do? I can't have this baby. I can't even tell Billy. He will want to marry me. This will kill my dad." I sobbed hysterically to my friend Bella.

My whole life flashed before my eyes, and it wasn't pretty. I didn't know what to do. I panicked and mentally wrote a dark future with this baby in it. Bella suggested I go back to the clinic and schedule an abortion.

"I don't know. I can't think straight, but that sounds scary. I can't think straight." I held my head in my hands.

Bella grabbed my hands in hers. "If you do this, you can just continue on with your life. You will never have to think about it again. I've done it. I know."

I looked up at her. I never knew this about her. I tried to hold back the shock in my face. "You never talk about it."

"See?" She smiled confidently. "Like I told you, you will never have to think about it again."

We went to the clinic and made an appointment. My mind was still jumbled, and I wasn't sure this was what I wanted. The procedure had to be done soon; I was near the time when I wouldn't have the choice anymore. I moved forward because the thought of telling anyone the news of my pregnancy made me shudder.

Bella drove me to the clinic out of town, while my brain fought my heart. My emotions were a roller coaster. *Or is this just the way a pregnant woman felt?* I didn't have time to figure it out.

I pushed on the glass double doors that led to a hallway and into a waiting room. Young girls looked up from their magazines then quickly stared back down. Their expressions said, *I know why you are here.* I signed in at the front desk and sat down with Bella. The room was cold and sterile, and I was shaking from the chill. Or maybe it was my nerves.

"Phylis Van Winkle." The nurse motioned for me to follow her.

I looked back at Bella. She smiled at me and mouthed, *I will be here.*

I walked into another waiting room. The nurse had me change into a gown. I had one last chance to back out. I couldn't imagine how I would take care of a baby right now. I was twenty years old, no job, living at home with my dad. There was no room in my life for this.

The nurse came back in and asked, "Do you want a valium to calm you down? It will help with the pain also." She held out her hand to dispense the medicine.

I grabbed it and downed it with some water. *I could use about five of those right now.* I lay on a gurney and waited.

The nurse wheeled me to a room that looked like a doctor's office. This one had a machine and big lamp overhead. The nurse held my hand and tried to be gentle with me, but I struggled through it.

"Make her keep still!" yelled the doctor.

The nurse looked at me with eyes pleading to do what he said.

I tried, but I wanted to die. I felt like I might.

In the recovery room, vanilla wafers and orange juice were provided to give us strength. The nurses made me and the other girls stay here so the staff could check on us to make sure we didn't collapse. My body ached in multiple ways. I felt like a part of me had died, and I just wanted to go home.

An hour later, I hobbled out to the front waiting room. My body was weak. I was glad Bella was there to drive me home. I just wanted this day to be over.

I told my dad I had a flu bug. I crawled into bed and stayed there for days. I felt numb. I couldn't even cry over the loss. I wasn't sure what had just happened to me, but I was sure I was damaged goods that no good man would ever want now. *I need my mom.*

I woke up with shooting pain through my abdomen. I sat straight up and grabbed my stomach to make it stop. As I pulled back the covers, the color of red splashed across my sheets. I was bleeding everywhere. I was in so much pain that I could hardly make it to the bathroom. The blood still gushed out. This was serious, and I couldn't fix things on my own.

I woke my dad up. "Dad, I need to go to the hospital now!"

"What is going on? You okay?" he asked as he dressed.

"I don't know. Maybe my appendix." I lied to get him moving. "Hurry!"

We arrived at the ER, and while my dad waited in the hallway, the doctor examined me right away. I explained to the doctor what I had done just weeks before.

"Phylis, you are hemorrhaging. They did not do the procedure well. If you had not come here within the hour, you could have bled to death. This is serious. We need to do an emergency D and C right away." The doctor assured me he would take good care of me. "I need to tell your father though."

"Why? You don't have to. I'm of age. Please don't tell him."

The doctor said he needed to inform my father because of the seriousness of the hemorrhaging. As he walked out the door, I saw my dad standing in the hallway, his face worried.

"Mr. Van Winkle, your daughter has made a mistake." The door shut behind him.

I didn't hear the rest of the conversation or see my dad's reaction. I did get a needle in my arm that shut out the last few hours.

I woke up to white curtains, white bedsheets, and sun filtering through my hospital room. My body felt better, but I was weak. I was in complete shock. What had just happened to my life? I stared at the ceiling and wondered what I would say to my father. Or what would he say to me. I felt ashamed on so many levels.

Just then Bella walked in. "What happened? I was so worried. I called your house. Your dad said you were here. When I asked him why, he said you could tell me." She was wide eyed with wonder.

I explained about the hemorrhaging and asked her about my dad. She said he sounded mad. After we talked for a bit, I sent her away. Exhausted, I fell into a deep sleep, and when I opened my eyes, my dad was sitting beside the bed, staring at me.

"Dad . . . I'm sorry." I started to tell him everything, but he stopped me.

"I brought you a change of clothes for when you leave tomorrow. I don't want to talk about it. You better never mention that boy's name in my house again." He looked away.

He thought Billy made me do this. Billy didn't even know. This was my fault. I would never get a chance to tell my dad that, because he couldn't handle any more of this. My mom . . . I couldn't reach out to her. I stuffed all these thoughts into the deep crevices of my soul, never to be spoken of again. I felt more alone than ever.

If God was disappointed in my choices before, he must hate me now.

CHAPTER 9

Broken Vows

TWO YEARS LATER, I WAS on my own again, living with one roommate in an apartment.

Considering all that had taken place, I wasn't dating seriously, and I was scared to get involved with anyone. My new job as an assistant secretary at a law firm meant no more hamburger flipping. Disco was my thing, and I couldn't wait to hit the bars on a Friday or Saturday night and dance to Donna Summer.

My favorite haunt was a local bar in town that the young crowd hung out at. My roommate and friends loved going there because we knew the bartenders. The nice ones would give us free drinks when we walked in, and usually one more during the night so we would stay longer. A few of the bartenders tried to date us, but we didn't want to get it twisted and have the romance end on a bad note, because then we would lose our favorite spot at the bar and have to find somewhere new.

Friday nights after work we dressed casually, usually a quick change into jeans. We grabbed something at home to eat or had the peanut and pretzel snacks at the bar. But Saturday nights were sparkles and minidresses with sequins or neon-colored tops paired with tight jeans and jewelry. On these nights, drinks were offered to us by all the men we knew. Some were friends, some wanted to be more than friends—and some we wanted and chased all night long. The pendulum never swung even. The evening would start out exciting, fun, and filled with the hope of catching the eye of the person you liked, then soon end with a deflated ego and second-guessing why you would go to such lengths for attention and affection.

Some evenings I caught a ride home with someone, stumbled into my apartment, and woke up miserable and lonely. Hungover, I repeated the process again the next weekend. Mom's drinking days flooded back to me.

During the week, I answered phones and typed up forms for the lawyers. On occasion, I drove with an attorney to a client's house. We would meet with a despondent soon-to-be ex-wife at her home. I saw dysfunction from the outside looking in and soon figured out that dysfunction did not discriminate. It took the wealthy hostage as much as the poor. Growing up I thought only people like my mom were dysfunctional, that my mom was unstable because of her situation or circumstances.

Then I met Mrs. B.

As we drove up a winding tree-filled road to a mansion that appeared in front of us, Mr. Matthews, my boss, had told me that Mrs. B. trusted me because I was nice to her. He had brought me along so I could take notes for him, and I was to mainly listen as Mrs. B. talked.

Then he said something that shocked me. "You are good at this—I've been watching you. You could become a paralegal someday."

Though awestruck by his compliment, I knew it was true. I was good at dealing with people. *This is a test I must pass*, I thought. I liked my job and wanted to continue to work there. I wasn't sure about my future at the firm, but I could figure that out later. I'd concentrate on what was in front of me.

We knocked on the door and were welcomed by a disheveled, white-robed Mrs. B. She had been crying. Her cheeks were red, her eyes puffy and swollen. She held a crumpled-up tissue in her hand and wiped her face when she greeted us.

"Oh my. I'm so sorry. I just couldn't muster up the energy to get dressed. Come in . . . please." She waved her arm for us to enter.

I took in the sight before me. The tall ceilings and pillars in the foyer. Marble flooring that shined so bright, it almost blinded me. The whole house was expansive and expensive. Mrs. B., however, was miserable. Her husband had walked out. He was in love with another woman and had come home one day and told her he wanted a divorce.

That was why we were there. We needed to divide up all the assets. He wanted to sell the house and didn't care where she ended up. She would get money to start over, but that wasn't the point. She loved her home, but this different life was being thrown on her like a moldy blanket.

Mr. Matthews and I sat on the brown leather couch, and I took out my notepad. I waited for him to start the conversation. I observed everything I could, to remember any detail he might want from me later.

Mr. Matthews opened his briefcase and took out papers for her to sign. When he reminded her that he needed her list for what she wanted to take with her from the house, she burst into tears.

"I want to stay here. Why do I have to leave? I didn't do anything except give him a good twenty years of my life. If he wants to start over, let him. Just let me be." She sobbed into her already wet tissue.

"Mrs. B., the facts aren't going to change. I've talked to his attorney several times. He wants to sell the house. We need you to let him know what things you want from the house. He is not going to change his mind." Mr. Matthews put his pen down and waited.

She glanced over at me. I stared back at her. I didn't want to show too much emotion, but I understood pain and was sympathetic to her situation. I'd had to move out of places when I wasn't ready.

She smiled. "I'm so glad you're here, Phylis. I don't know why, but you are such a calming force. What would you take if you were me? What would you do?" She was genuinely asking my inexperienced opinion.

I looked over at Mr. Matthews, who nodded at me.

I tried to stay encouraging. "Well, I'm no expert in this, but I think I would take the most important things. Things that you could put in your new home. Maybe we could start with this room first. Then later today you could walk through each room and think about what else you might want."

Mrs. B. held my arm in hers while she looked at Mr. Matthews. "You're right. I was overwhelmed thinking about all the things in the house at once. I could start with one room at a time. See? This is why I love this girl."

Mr. Matthews grinned at me

I just passed a test, I thought.

Later that night, I told my friends about the experience as we were sitting at our local hangout, sipping our drinks and swaying to the disco music blaring from the speakers.

"Honestly, guys, it was the best day ever. When we got back in the car, Mr. Matthews said I acted so well, just like he knew I would. He said if he had gone there by himself, he wouldn't have been so sympathetic." Just as I finished my sentence, *he* walked through the door.

A gorgeous, tall, dark, and handsome guy whom I had never seen before. My stomach churned out feelings my heart couldn't keep up with.

"Who is that?" I tried to play it cool, as if asking out of curiosity, not a need to know, but my friends laughed.

Sadie nudged my shoulder. "Ooh, somebody has an instant crush."

I hadn't felt this way in a long time, and had to look away so he didn't catch me staring. I didn't want to be involved with anyone. I wanted to focus on myself and my career.

Just then Sadie grabbed my shoulder and whispered in my ear, "He's coming over!"

I took a swig of my drink to calm my nerves.

"Hello, ladies." He stared directly at me, even though he had addressed the table. Everyone said "hi" back, watching what would happen next.

"I'm Dax. Do you want to dance?"

He brushed his hand on my arm. I nodded yes and reached for his outstretched hand. His big and manly hand. He was tall, at least six feet. I followed him onto the dance floor. The room was dark, with the strobe light flickering around in a circle above the ceiling. The multicolored lights shone down on us, as if we were the dancing stars on stage. His dark-brown eyes never stopped penetrating through me. I felt naked, exposed to his gaze. This feeling was one I had a love-hate struggle with. I loved guys who knocked me off balance. Who seemed dangerous. But I hated that I felt unsafe at times.

We locked gazes as we moved in unison to the music. He was an amazing dancer, and I liked that we synced so well. When the song ended, he walked me back to the table.

"Mind if I join you guys?" He looked at my girlfriends, who were more than happy to oblige.

He pulled up a chair and waved to the bartender to make him another drink. We talked and laughed and had deep conversation of current events. I danced with him a few more times, and then his friends trickled in.

"I'm going back to the bar, but come see me before you leave, okay?"

His gaze disarmed me. I said a whispered *okay* before I watched him walk away.

My friends squealed in the corner at my awkwardness. "You really like him. Are you going to stop by and see him before you leave?"

"I guess. I don't really know him. What is wrong with me?" I shook my head, as if to clear the dusty cobwebs.

Before I left, I stopped to say goodbye. He invited me back to his friend's house, which felt safe enough since I knew the friend. I told my group where I was going and said I would call them in the morning.

Dax and I ended up talking until four in the morning. He was unlike anyone I had met before. He was a man's man all the way. I loved his masculinity. He drove me home and asked to see me again.

"Would you like to take a ride to the city with me? I'm heading up to Sausalito next Saturday. I would love the company."

How could I say no to those eyes?

Inseparable for the next few months, we enjoyed social gatherings, but when we were alone, he often became quiet and distant. I wrote it off as him being shy or just tired.

Things were coasting along with work, I had a grown-up boyfriend, and I had moved by myself to a new apartment. Life was finally stabilizing.

On the other hand, Mom's life continued to be chaotic. She was working, but she was also partying just as hard and hanging around with a new set of friends that I didn't know.

Mom had gotten the job at the deli in San Jose. She'd found a small studio apartment close enough to the deli that she could walk to work. She still hadn't learned to drive, but she finally bought a phone, so occasionally she would call. She talked about her hard life. She never had time to give me advice or visit my sister. Her life was about survival—hers, not ours. She persisted in drinking at bars, and she would tell me about how the bartenders watched out for her and protected her.

I now understood this in an odd way. I also frequented a couple bars in which the bartenders told me whom I should watch out for or when I should go home because I was drunk.

I hadn't heard from Mom in about a month. I hadn't expected the phone call I got in the middle of the morning.

"Hello? Are you Phylis?" asked the person on the other end.

"Yes, who is this?" I rubbed the sleep out of my eyes.

"This is John from the 7-Eleven store in San Jose. Your mom came running in here tonight, all bloody. We saw her jump out of a car. She said the man was trying to kill her. We tried to call the police and ambulance, but she refused. We drove her home, and she said to call you."

He talked so fast I could hardly believe what he was telling me. "What! Is she okay? What do you mean, all bloody? How bloody?" My brain couldn't handle what was being thrown at me. I wished I had never picked up the phone.

Why did she always expect me to fix it?

I threw on some jeans and a T-shirt, grabbed the car keys, and drove up to her place. My mind raced to all kinds of bad scenarios on the drive up. I pulled up to the curb outside her apartment early in the morning, quiet and peaceful outside. I knocked quietly so as not to disturb anyone nearby who might still be sleeping. No answer. I tried the door. It was unlocked. I slowly pushed it open and saw Mom lying on her bed, facing away from me. I could see only the top of her head.

"Mom?" I tiptoed toward her.

I stopped dead as my eyes grazed her face. She was indeed a bloody mess. Both her eyes were almost swollen shut. A huge gash slashed her forehead, which I was sure needed stitches. Her lips were cut and puffy. The rest of her body had bruises, probably from falling out of the car.

"Oh my God! Mom!" I knelt beside her.

She grabbed my hand and winced. "Phylis . . . help me," she cried in pain and sadness. She couldn't move.

I couldn't fix this.

"Mom, I need to call an ambulance. This is crazy. What happened? You need to report this to the police!" I half yelled, half pleaded.

She reached for my arm.

I knew what would come next.

"No. You can fix this. It's not that bad. I will be okay. Just clean me up. I will rest a few days and be fine. I'm so embarrassed. I knew I shouldn't have gotten in the car with him." Then she told me what happened.

Another night at the bar, another stranger to flirt with, only this time he turned dangerous.

"I had a feeling, you know. My intuition told me not to go. I needed a ride home. I didn't want to walk. He said he could take me. As soon as I got in the car, I felt weird. Then he starts driving and telling me he's going to kill me, dump my body in the Los Gatos Hills, where no one can find me. He punched my face. I fought him off. I went to grab for the door handle and realized there wasn't one. I just kept reaching into the empty pocket where the handle should be. Something snapped, and the door flew open. I jumped out and ran to the store. The people there were so nice. They brought me home." She panted from reliving the nightmare.

I found washcloths and some medicine and started wiping away all the blood to see where her wounds were. The worst one was her forehead.

"Mom, I can't fix this. You really need stitches." I pleaded with her to go to the hospital.

She vehemently refused. With the biggest bandages I could find, I made a butterfly stitch to close the wound.

We were such a dysfunctional family. Why couldn't I stand up to her and demand she see a doctor? The more I dealt with her issues, the more I saw why my thinking was damaged.

I cleaned her up, fed her some soup, and promised to be back the next day to check on her. I told her to call me if she felt worse. I knew she wouldn't. She would suffer it out until I came back later.

I drove back to town and told Dax what happened. He comforted me in his big, strong arms. As I dressed for our date that night, I thought, *I need to worry only about my life, not hers.* This relationship was a whirlwind romance, and Dax and I were falling in love. I wanted to stay in that feel-good bubble forever.

My mom recovered, vowing never to drink again, only to end up in the same bar months later—with a brave attitude that she would find the guy who'd beat her and have him arrested. She said she did see him one night, but froze as he looked over at her. By the time she'd found her voice to tell the bartender, the man had bolted out the door—never to be seen again.

I vowed to Mom I would not help her again if she put herself in dangerous situations. I didn't even believe myself when I said it.

Dax took me to dinner one night at a fancy restaurant. We had a lively conversation about his family and how much I loved them. Just then he leaned in and pulled a small black box out of his pocket.

"I love you and want to spend my life with you. Will you marry me?"

I heard clapping in the restaurant.

"Yes!" I squealed and jumped up to hug him and put that ring on my finger.

His family loved me. I loved them. My dad loved Dax. My mom couldn't be bothered to be a part of my life, and I pretended she didn't exist. Dax was my family now. This was what family felt like. I imagined going to his parents' house on Sundays for dinner. We did that sometimes now, but I looked into the future, thinking of the children we would have. They would run around playing, and I would be helping his mom in the kitchen. We would go home to our own little house. It would be fixed up warm and comfy, and life would be perfect.

New Year's Eve approached, and his parents thought it was the perfect time to celebrate our engagement. Dax's entire family was there, along with my dad and my siblings, but my mom had not been invited. I knew that if I invited her, she would create a scene. Better not to scare his family. Let them think I was normal.

Balloons, table settings with champagne, and poppers highlighted the midnight celebrations. I couldn't remember a time when I had been happier.

Months had gone by since that beautiful evening. We worked during the week and partied on the weekends, my drug use now more sophisticated than before—we used one hundred dollar bills to roll up and snort the cocaine. We hung out in nicer houses than when I was a teen in my friends' parents' home. Nothing seemed wrong except those quiet times alone with my thoughts.

I was tired of waking up hungover on Saturday mornings. I wanted more for my life. I dreamed of traveling, testing out things I had never done before. The people I hung out with didn't inspire me to do those things—they were happy with the status quo. My bucket list of dreams just kept growing. Then I thought how selfish this thinking was. I was in love, engaged to be married. I should be content with the way my life was turning out. The dreams would have to be tucked away for another time as I planned my wedding day.

One late afternoon when I headed to Dax's to make dinner, I stopped dead when I saw a suitcase by the front door. I walked into the apartment to find Dax putting some things in a backpack.

"What's going on?" I hurriedly put the groceries on the counter.

"I'm leaving for a few days. I need to clear my head." He stuffed clothes into the bag.

"When were you going to tell me? Or were you just going to leave before I got here?" I was mad because I already knew the answer.

He tried to explain that it was him, not me. That I needed to calm down and trust him. I didn't trust anyone, for this very reason. Something had been brewing for weeks, but I'd chosen to ignore it, as I wasn't good at confrontations. I saw what had happened when my parents confronted each other. Truth was, I was scared to communicate with any man, and I shut down. Now, it boiled to the surface.

"When will you be back?" I was terrified he wouldn't return.

"I'm not sure, probably a week. Don't worry. I will be back soon. I just can't stay here right now. It's too complicated to talk about." He didn't even look at me.

"You're supposed to be talking to me though. I need to know what's going on in your mind. I'm going to be your wife." Tears flowed down my cheeks.

This face was getting tired of them. Why did men always leave me crying?

My pleading went unanswered. He quickly kissed me and walked out the door. I walked into the kitchen, put the groceries away, and left. I silently prayed, begged, to make him come back and love me.

He did come back a week later. He still wouldn't talk about what had unhinged him. We settled into an uneasy truce. Then I was confronted with a question I had no answer for.

I was walking to my car from work one day, when I saw a mutual friend of ours.

"Hey! Haven't seen you around for a bit. You doing okay? I heard about your broken engagement. I'm so sorry." He stood there with a pitiful look.

I was speechless. *Did I just hear him right?*

"Um . . . I'm good. And still engaged." I looked down at the engagement ring on my finger.

He backed away from me as if he'd just informed me of something I was not aware of.

"Where did you hear that nonsense?" I was annoyed that someone had spread rumors about us.

"Dax . . . he told me a couple of days ago. I'm so sorry. I . . . maybe I heard him wrong." He tried to comfort me by taking it back.

I shouldn't have been shocked, since things hadn't been the same since he'd been back home. He didn't share anything with me anymore. But I needed to hear it from him. How dare he tell people without telling me first. Did he honestly think in this small town that people wouldn't talk? I felt exposed. As I moved to my car, I was sure every person who walked past me knew. I drove through Gilroy, positive the drivers in the passing cars were staring at me, feeling sorry for me. I approached Dax's apartment, ready to blast him.

His car was not there, so I didn't even get out.

That night, I walked into our favorite bar with an attitude, positive I would see him. I would not let him make excuses anymore.

He saw me walk in. He was standing there, drink in hand, looking as cool and sexy as when I'd first met him. But I had the strength to know I needed more than a pretty face.

As I paced up to him, he smirked at me. A condescending kind of smirk. Now I was straight out pissed.

"What are looking so mad at?" he mocked.

I stared directly at him and held his gaze. "I'm going to ask you this once. You better tell me the truth. Did you tell Joe that we weren't engaged anymore?"

"When did you see him? What did he say to you?" He asked questions so he didn't have to answer mine.

"Just answer my question first." I glared at him.

He looked away and then back at me. He took a drink. "Yeah. Sorry. It just slipped out. I was going to tell you tonight. There are just some things in my life right now . . . I can't get married. Don't ask me why. I love you. I just can't marry you."

There it was.

I didn't need to hear any more. I stomped out of the bar and drove back to my apartment. I walked into a dark, quiet room and didn't bother turning the lights on. I sat there with my jumbled thoughts. Half an hour went by, and I heard a car door close. I wanted it to be Dax. I had prayed he would follow me out of the bar. Beg me to forgive him. Say he had changed his mind. That at any moment he would come running up the stairs, saying it was all a mistake.

Instead it was my girlfriends coming up the stairs. I heard their platform shoes plunking up the steps.

"Phylis, open the door. We know your home, sweetie. We heard what happened." They'd come to rescue me.

Thank God for friends. I slowly opened the door. They wrapped their arms around me. We cried. We laughed. We got high. I didn't know where I was going from here. Maybe I was doomed to be single forever.

Mom was probably right. You couldn't trust a man or life. Both would always let you down.

CHAPTER 10

What Is Family?

DAX ASKED ME FOR THE engagement ring back.

I was visiting his sister at her house one day because I still cared for his family. They still cared for me too and were devastated that Dax had broken up with me. He wouldn't tell them why either. I stayed in touch with them to let them know I was holding out hope that maybe someday we would get back together.

His sister and I weren't expecting him to come over. When she heard his car pull up outside, she thought it was a sign he would ask me to come back. His sister opened the door, but he wouldn't come in.

My heart pounded like it always did when I saw him.

He motioned for me to come out. "Can I talk to you for a second?" He held the door open so I could meet him.

His sister smiled at me hopefully, and I tried to remain calm as my shaking legs walked me to the front door. I wandered with him to the courtyard of the house.

"How are you? You look great." He stood there, hands in pockets.

"I'm okay. What do you want to talk about?" I just couldn't do small talk right then.

"I hate to do this to you. I know I told you to keep the ring, but . . . I really need it back." He looked at the ring I had yet to take off my finger.

I had put it on my right hand so as not to pretend I was engaged anymore. I was hoping someday it would end up back on my left-hand ring finger. His demand was the nail in the engagement coffin.

It was over. I had nothing else to tie me to him. I threw it at him and ran back into his sister's house. I cried for the last time over him that day.

I'll show him. Someone will marry me, and he will be sorry.

I met Bo at a party at his house in town. Just another fun night on a Friday. A friend had told me about this party, and I'd known Bo since childhood but hadn't seen him in years. Bo Logan had been friends with my brother as a teen. He had always been kind and polite.

My friend and I sauntered through the door, and as soon as I saw Bo, I felt comfortable. We caught up on old times for the rest of the night. He was intelligent and easy to talk to. I was entering my midtwenties, and I'd found that intellect was important for me in a relationship. We started dating right away.

Afraid of commitment, I was in no hurry to get serious. I was desperately trying to find my way in this life, a different path than the one my mom had taken. My fear was that I would repeat the bad patterns I had grown up with.

Bo was responsible and reliable, and he owned his own home. He was not Dax. I was done with handsome bad boys. Bo was cute and nice, and I needed nice in my life.

Job-wise, I had switched from the law firm to a real estate company. I was a wonderful asset as a receptionist, not so great as a typist. I easily memorized all the names of the regular clients we dealt with, and I learned about their families and personal likes and dislikes. The bosses invited me and my coworker to drinks and dinner with some of their best clients. I got a glimpse of how the privileged lived, which led me to consider my future. I wanted the finer things in life. I wasn't sure they were within my reach, but I was taking mental notes. I watched how the women walked and talked. I learned their movements. They were refined. I was rough around the edges, but I had a knack for being funny to divert my weaknesses. The clients invited me to more of their social outings, so I upgraded my wardrobe.

Though Bo already had a roommate, he encouraged me to move into his house. None of his other friends owned homes, so his three-bedroom, one-story house, with a good-sized backyard, was the perfect party house. I mixed the drug-and-alcohol-infused nights at Bo's with the work-associated swanky parties on the other side of town. I lived in two different worlds and enjoyed them both.

I'd been living with Bo for four months when I woke up and immediately recognized the signals my body was giving me. I was pregnant.

The timing couldn't be worse. I was not sure he was my forever love. This was what happened when you played "pretend family." I thought it would be okay to live with him, to find out if I really wanted to spend the rest of my life with him. Now that choice was being made for me. I took a pregnancy test as soon as I made it home from the office, as I had to see a positive test before telling Bo. I waited for the stick to tell me the truth. For a moment I thought maybe it would be negative, but the red line was there.

I sat on the couch, waiting for Bo to come home from work. I heard the car door shut and watched him walk up the driveway.

"Hey there, beautiful. You're home early." He popped a kiss onto my cheek.

I felt sick, and it wasn't from my pregnancy. I didn't know how he would take this news. Would I be kicked out, only to start over on my own? One thing I knew—I would keep this baby. I would never again go through what had happened before. I would have this baby with or without him.

"Can you just sit down for a minute? I have something to tell you." I patted the cushion next to me. "So . . . I didn't expect this to happen at all. I'm so sorry, and I don't know how you are going to take this news . . . " I couldn't get the words out.

He smiled.

"I'm pregnant." I showed him the stick.

His smile grew bigger. He was not shocked or mad. Not the expression I expected.

"Honey, that's great!" He came in for the biggest hug.

I took a deep breath of relief, now excited about this journey we were embarking on.

"I've been wanting to ask you something." He grasped my hands and leaned into me. "I have an heirloom ring waiting with my mom. I want to marry you. Now I'm sure of it."

He kissed me, and we started making marriage plans.

I continued to work and told my best friend from the office and a few other friends but swore them to secrecy. Bo told his family, mostly so he could get the ring from his mother. Wedding plans surged ahead full force, with Bo's big Italian family taking over all the tasks.

My mom lived somewhere in San Jose again. She had lost her job at the deli, which had been followed with getting evicted from her apartment. I couldn't keep up with her nomad life. When she did occasionally drift into town, I sometimes met up with her. She was exhausting to be around, as nothing about her life was joyful.

I didn't want to share my news with her, but I told my dad, and he seemed guardedly happy. I thought he was worried about my pregnancy, considering the trauma I'd been through from the abortion.

I didn't share his concerns. Until at work one day when I needed to use the bathroom. I ran into the restroom to find out I was spotting blood. My face drained as I thought the worst. I told my bosses I was sick and rushed home. I called Bo and told him to meet me at the doctors.

We were waiting in a clinic office when the doctor came in. "I have done another pregnancy test since the last time you were in here. After looking over the ultrasound, I'm sorry to tell you both that there is no viable pregnancy. It seems you had a miscarriage. I'm so sorry." He looked from the paperwork to us, then back to the paperwork.

This had to be the worst news he gave couples. Ironically, I worried more about him than myself. A sense of calm settled over me. Now we could slow down this relationship and see where it was going. I was also heartbroken, as I already felt like a mom. I had been ready to take on this new role.

Bo couldn't have been sweeter or more attentive. I stayed in bed for a few days to recover, and he brought me hot tea, cookies, and anything else I needed so I could rest. I thought I was falling deeply in love with him, though I was not ready to commit to marriage.

A few days later we came home from work at the same time. I was ready to share with him how my heart needed time to process a future with him. I told him I wanted to wait to get married, that he was not obligated to marry me just because I'd been pregnant.

"Are you kidding? I wasn't marrying you just because you were pregnant. I love you and want to spend my life with you." He hugged me tight.

This should have been a pivotal moment. I finally had someone who really loved me and wanted to take care of me. Then why did I feel smothered and out of control? I couldn't find the voice to explain that I needed this wedding train to slow down.

"We can wait for just a bit so we don't have to rush the marriage. Then maybe we can plan a little better for the whole thing." I tried to be uplifting.

But he was giddy over all the plans. "My whole family has everything planned out. Mom and my aunts are making all the food. We're having the reception in my sister's backyard. You just worry about getting your dress and flowers."

He left the room to grab something to eat. I was left with my words floating above my head like a cartoon bubble. I tried to build up my excitement, but I felt doomed to fail. I couldn't put my finger on it, but something was not right.

The next few months zoomed by. A friend's mother made my wedding dress, a simple, beautiful satin floor-length dress. His cousins, aunts, sister, and mom, Norma, joined together to make the upcoming day wonderful.

We picked a tiny church in town. We met with the pastor, and he asked us a few questions. Apparently, we passed the test. In a few days we would be husband and wife.

Why does it feel like my funeral? I wished I had the kind of mom I could bounce off my indecisiveness. Occasionally I spotted Mom in town when she returned to her local haunts to see her drinking buddies, but she still lived out of town.

Bo's father had passed away a few years earlier but Bo's mom and dad had been friends with my mom and dad when we were babies. Norma asked if my mom was coming to the wedding. "It would be nice to see your mom again if she's up for coming." She tried to be upbeat for my sake.

Half the time, I didn't even know how to reach my mother. The phone numbers she gave me were for other people's phones. They'd tell me she wasn't there anymore. I didn't bother trying to find her. I didn't want her there.

My father would walk me down the aisle. My siblings and some of my cousins would be there. That was family now.

My wedding day arrived. The dress was beautiful. The flowers were sweet and simple. Half of Bo's relatives were busily making the last-minute preparations.

I waited in the back room for my time to walk down the aisle. My dad poked his head in to check on me. "Last chance to back out." He laughed, thinking he was making a joke.

"I'll be out in a minute, Dad. I need to check my makeup one last time." I smiled to hide my pain.

The door closed, and I engaged in a conversation with someone I couldn't see.

Is this what I should be doing? Something doesn't feel right, I said to myself, quietly waiting for the God in the sky to answer me. Nothing. I was by myself. I must decide now. My time was up.

I walked out the door, wrapped my arm through my dad's, and heard that quiet voice with each step: *I don't think this is right . . . I don't think this is right*. Too late. I was at the altar.

Our married life started out with his roommate asking if he could stay with us until he found his own place. I wasn't on board, but this was Bo's house first. I obliged, but I was looking forward to some privacy once he left.

The house had been Bo's bachelor pad before we married, and his friends weren't used to calling now before coming over or limiting their time here. Most days I drove home from work and saw his friends already waiting in their cars for us to arrive. They wanted to party and hang out. I wanted to cook a nice dinner for us and talk about our day. Bo tried to compromise.

Some of those friends didn't like our married life.

"Bo, can they please call before they just stop by? I'm trying to make dinner for us, and I don't have enough food for everyone. I want to be alone with you, not with a bunch of men here every day!"

He tried to please all of us. And since we all liked getting high, I didn't fuss much about his friends tagging along. I just didn't want to get high during the week, when I had to head to the office the next day. I would get drunk while they got high on weed. Dinner would sometimes never get finished, and we'd order out instead.

Soon the roommate moved out, and I thought we would become the newlyweds we were meant to be. I anticipated us growing closer and leaning on each other for everything. I wasn't expecting a third party to join our marriage.

After work, I saw Bo pacing through the front window as I stepped up to our front door. I entered the kitchen, and he unloaded the news.

"Honey, come sit down. We need to talk about some things. It's kind of important." He pulled me to the couch in the living room.

"What is going on? You're scaring me. You look weird. Did you lose your job or something?" I was trying to guess how bad the news would be.

"It's not entirely bad news. You know my mom was living with her boyfriend in Winnemucca, Nevada, right? Well, the bad news is, my mom broke up with him and is moving home."

I wondered why this made him anxious. "I'm sorry about that. Is she okay?"

"Oh, well, you know, she is sad, but she told me she's excited to move back home."

"That's good. She will be close to family. When is she moving back?" I smiled, happy he would have his mom close by again, as he was close to his mother.

"That's the part I need to talk to you about. She is moving in with us." He looked away nervously.

He couldn't have just said what I thought he did. "What do you mean? Moving into our house? We just got the house back to ourselves. You mean moving in until she finds an apartment?" I could handle a month or two of inconvenience.

"No." He cleared his throat.

"There's something I didn't tell you completely. I told you I owned this house, right? Well, I do. The part I didn't tell you was that I bought it with my mom. She owns half the house. Technically, this is her house too."

I didn't know what to say. He'd lied to me. "What does that mean? She's going to live here forever with us? Are you crazy? I just got you to myself, and now another person is moving back in?" I launched up from the couch. I needed to move away from him before I slapped him.

"I'm going out for a bit. I need some air. I'll be back later." I called my girlfriend Jesse. I asked her to meet me at our favorite bar and then grabbed my car keys and headed out the door.

We slid onto the barstools and ordered drinks. "How could he do this to me? I want to kill him. He lied to me." I chugged back my beer.

"What are you going to do?" Jesse asked.

"What choice do I have? He's my husband. I would look like a horrible person if I left now. I'm just so sick of men not being truthful with me. I don't want a mother-in-law living with us!" I ran my hands through my hair, rubbing the sides of my forehead. I was getting a migraine. *Maybe it's a tumor and I can just die from this world.*

Norma Logan moved into our house a month later. A sweet woman, she unpacked her belongings into a spare room and put the rest of her things in storage.

"I don't want to be a problem for you two." She smiled at me.

I liked her—I just didn't want her knowing my business. We would have to work together if we were all going to live under the same roof.

Norma helped around the house and did most of the grocery shopping and cleaning. That freed Bo and me to spend time with our friends. Instead of having friends over, I met mine at a restaurant or their house, as there was no space to talk privately in my home. Occasionally, friends would come over, and Norma would make snacks and drinks for us.

I would grin at my girlfriends because it felt like a mom serving her kids snacks after school. I didn't need a mom doing this for me at my age. It was annoying. Resentment built inside me as her presence grew more intrusive.

One evening after I had gone out for drinks with friends, I came home to her pouty face. I walked into the kitchen to see her tapping her fingers on the table.

"Where have you been? And why didn't you and Bo come home after work?" she questioned, clearly annoyed.

"We went out with our friends. I told him to tell you we weren't coming home straight after work. Did you make dinner?" I looked over at the pots on the stove, filled with food.

"I made a nice dinner, and now it's ruined. You should have told me. I've been waiting for you guys since five o'clock." She fumed.

I didn't want a mommy making me dinner, and I certainly didn't need to tell her what time I was coming home from work. *I have done quite well without a mom until now. I don't need a mom at this age.*

The next week she gleefully waited in the kitchen for my return. "Look what I did for you today! I rearranged all the cupboards back to the way I used to have them when I first lived here. It's so much more organized this way!" She ecstatically showed me.

I opened each door slowly, gazing over dishes, glasses, spices, all in different cupboards than I had placed them, which shouldn't have been a big deal. My face heated up. I wanted to be grateful; instead I felt violated. There was no room for two women in this house. *One of us must go.*

"It's really nice. Excuse me. I need to go to my room and change." I trounced past her in a huff, feeling guilty because I'd hurt her feelings. I closed the door to my bedroom, burst out in tears, and plopped onto my bed. The conversation I would have with Bo would tear him apart. How did you ask a son to choose between his wife and his mom? But choose he must. It had been five months of living like this. I couldn't do one more day.

Later, as I lay on the bed, I overheard Norma talking in low tones to Bo. Probably telling him what a mean daughter-in-law I was. His loafers then squeaked on the hallway floor, and he opened the bedroom door.

He sat beside me. "You okay? My mom said you seemed irritated. She told me about the cupboards. You know she is only trying to help." He pleaded his mom's case.

"I don't need her help!" I said too loudly. He was taking her side, and I didn't want to be here anymore. "Bo, I'm reminded daily that this is your mother's house. There is no room for me here." I had mentally moved out.

This was not the marriage I'd thought it would be. I had made a terrible mistake. He loved his mother first, and I couldn't compete with that. I was the intruder.

"I'm moving out. I'll go back home to my dad's until I find someplace to live. I can't do this anymore."

"No! Wait. I can fix this. Please don't say that. I love you."

And there it was. I had to come to terms with what I had been feeling since I walked down the aisle to say, "I do." I didn't love him that same way. Not the way he loved me. I needed to be released from this contract. I didn't want to break his heart, but my heart was slowly dying from emptiness. I agreed to stay the night and pack tomorrow.

The next morning, I woke up late, since it was a Saturday and I had the whole day to pack. I treaded out to the kitchen to grab some water. Bo and his mother sat at the kitchen table. She looked up at me and told me to sit with them. I didn't want to share my feelings with them—I wanted to get my water and go back to my room.

But even more, I didn't want to cause trouble, so I sat.

"Bo tells me you want to leave. Please don't do that. We can figure something out. I was just trying to be the best mom to both of you. I know you don't understand what a family is since you have never had one. Maybe you just need more time so we can show you." She patted my arm condescendingly.

She was attacking my childhood? I pulled away. "I may not know what a family is, but I know this is not the family I had in mind." I rose from the table, rushed to the bedroom, and packed a bag. I told Bo I would be back when I needed more things. I left him crying and headed to Dad's house.

Dad looked up from his newspaper and saw the suitcase by my side. "What is going on? You okay?" He had been through this before, and he knew the signs of a broken marriage. He didn't want that for me.

I took the spare room since Dad had taken over the big bedroom once I'd moved out. I unpacked then met him in the living room. I told Dad what had happened, and he just shook his head. I knew I was a disappointment to him even if he didn't say the words out loud.

Bo came by in tears a few days later. "I can't do this. Tell me what you want. I want to die. Please come back home."

"Give me time. I'm not sure what I need right now." I felt guilty, as I didn't want to be responsible if something happened to him. I agreed to meet with him the following weekend.

My dad had gone out of town to stay with his girlfriend, so I invited Bo over for a talk. Part of me still loved him, and we spent the night together.

Two months later I discovered I was pregnant. *God has a sick sense of humor.*

I quit my job, since Bo and I decided I would stay home after the baby was born. We figured the only way we could make this marriage work was if we moved into an apartment away from his mom.

His family threw me a baby shower. They invited my mom, but she didn't show up. She couldn't be bothered with my life if it didn't revolve around her. My sister was there—we giggled at all the little baby clothes.

I loved being pregnant, but I was gaining weight fast. Bo was loving but at times distant. He slept on the couch, saying he was trying to give me my rest. I was aware of how puffy I had become. I was not the same wife he'd married. I looked different. I sat in the baby's room most days and wondered what life would be like as a new mom. I wanted to do it differently than my mom, though I held a fear I might not be able to handle this.

At two o'clock one morning, I woke up to a wet bed and pain in my gut. My water had broken. I called to Bo, and we grabbed my bag and rushed to the hospital, thirty minutes away in San Jose. I'd started labor, and I hoped I would be out of labor soon. I had gained sixty pounds with this baby and was ready to meet him or her.

After twenty hours of hard labor, the doctors decided to do a cesarean delivery. My beautiful baby boy, Linton Miles, was born at a whopping nine pounds, thirteen ounces. I was exhausted but blissful. Giving birth was the most amazing experience of my life. I loved him the minute I laid eyes on him.

I had to stay in the hospital for four days to heal from my surgery. Linton was sleepy when they put him in my arms, and he never ate much. I wrote it off to going through such a hard labor. By the third day a nurse let me know that he needed to eat more.

"Your baby is the most disruptive in the nursery. You need to nurse him longer." She shoved Linton's head to my chest and proceeded to inform me how to feed him properly.

"I understand. I will try harder to wake him up to feed him." I wanted her out of my room and away from my baby. I put Linton to my breast. He nursed for a few minutes, then fell asleep. I held him and stroked his hair.

"I won't let anything happen to you. I will protect you. I love you, Linton," I whispered as I kissed his cheek.

One of the nicer nurses came in to take Linton back to the nursery. My intuition told me something was wrong, and when my sister stopped by to visit, I said, "Sissy, I'm worried. Can you please go check on Linton? I have a bad feeling."

I waited for her to come back to tell me I was a paranoid mom and my boy was fine, sleeping peacefully in the nursery. Instead, she walked in, fear in her expression.

"Sissy, I can't find him. I walked around twice to investigate the nursery. I don't see him."

"What do you mean? Where is he?" I tried to get out of bed, but my sore body wouldn't let me.

Just then a doctor entered. "There's an issue with your son. We are running some tests right now. We will keep you informed as soon as we know." He walked out.

The room spun. I couldn't breathe. I needed to call Bo. What was happening?

The next two hours nurses and doctors rotated in to update me on my son's condition. By the time Bo arrived, they had called in a heart surgeon. He informed us that Linton had stopped breathing in the nursery twice. They'd revived him and ran test after test. They discovered that he needed emergency open-heart surgery. That was, if they could keep him alive long enough to transport him to Stanford Medical Center, where the top heart surgeons could operate.

"We need to take him right now while he is stable. Would you like us to wheel you out to say goodbye?" Dr. Grady gently asked us.

I was still too weak from my cesarean to walk, so they pushed my chair right up to his gurney. I grabbed Linton's arm and cried. "Mama loves you, honey. You're going to be okay. I love you so much. I'll see you real soon, okay?" Tears flowed down my cheeks. I couldn't believe they were taking my baby boy away from me. I touched his face.

Bo hugged him and said his loving goodbyes also. Then they wheeled Linton off to the ambulance. We were told the doctor would call me as soon as the surgery was over. They had to open him up to see what they were dealing with before they could tell me how dire the situation was.

Hours went by. Bo had long since gone back home. He had contemplated staying, but the room held only a chair to sleep in. I wanted him to stay, but I didn't feel I should need to beg him.

I lay there thinking about how I had gotten to this place. I was twenty-six years old. I had been through so much. Things should have settled down so I could enjoy a normal life.

Is there such a thing? I wondered, Maybe my mom was right. Life always disappointed you.

As I waited for the doctor to call, the other new mom in my room had her baby come in to nurse. I glanced over at the loving exchange taking place between them, and anger raged within me. I didn't want to be in a room with someone who seemed to have it all. I pulled the curtain between us so I could have privacy.

The phone rang a few minutes later.

"Phylis?" It was Dr. Grady.

"Yes, it's me."

"Let me start by saying the surgery is over. Your son was born with congenital heart disease. There are usually about five major things that can go wrong when the heart is forming. Most of the time, if it is one or two things, we can fix that through surgery. Your son had several things wrong. We have done all we can, and now we wait. But I must tell you, it is not looking good." He was calm and steady as he delivered the news.

He went into more specific medical detail of Linton's condition, but I couldn't speak. *My son might die.* Those were the only words that stuck. I hung up the phone and called Bo. What I would have given to have a mom to comfort me. I had never felt more alone and scared.

I needed to be with my son.

I was supposed to be at home resting. The hospital had made me promise—the doctor would release me early if I stayed in bed at home. Bo still had to work, though he had taken several days off already and gone to see Linton. He'd taken pictures on his camera and had them developed in an hour so I could see my son.

I couldn't stand being away from Linton, so I called my dad. "Dad, come and get me and take me up to the hospital."

"Aren't you supposed to stay at home? They said no long car rides or anything that would tire you out."

"Dad, come and get me. I will put a pillow on my tummy. Then it won't hurt my stitches. I need to go see Linton now!"

We drove the hour up to the hospital. Bumps on the road made me flinch from the pain, but I needed to see my son.

The hospital was so big and expansive I almost got lost as we made our way to the NICU. I walked in and saw a row of babies. All in beds, all hooked up to machines. I walked over to Linton, and the nurses greeted me.

"You have the sweetest baby. And he's so big! We are taking good care of him. Anything you need, just let us know. Here, come over here and sit." The nurse pulled up a chair next to my son's gurney-like bed, raised to arm level so that the nurses could care for him easier as they injected medicines and took vitals.

The unit whirled with doctors and nurses. I learned that they assessed the patients each day and had meetings to review the progress or decline of each baby. The team was fully invested in each case. A calmness enveloped me, knowing that Linton was being well taken care of.

Seeing him hooked up to machines was another story. I held his tiny hand and watched his face turn different hues of red. He was having seizures. I was told he didn't feel them because of his medication, but I didn't believe the doctors.

Over time, many of our relatives from both sides of our family showed up. Bo and I took turns letting them know about any progress, which changed every day.

My mother came to Bo's sister's house, where we often all met at the end of the day. Mom was a complete mess as she hugged me.

"I can't believe this is happening to me. This is the worst thing that has ever happened." She was sobbing.

I pulled away from her. "This isn't happening to you, Mom. It's happening to me." I walked away from her to get a drink of water. I needed some space.

"Well, of course. That's what I meant. Don't be so sensitive. I'm here for you—you know that." She glanced at the relatives, who stared back at her.

They knew what she meant. They each gave me a hug of solidarity.

My mother didn't go to the hospital to see Linton. "I just can't go see him, honey. It's too much. You know how I hate hospitals." She looked solemnly at me.

I wished I could have the luxury of bowing out on life when it got tough and uncomfortable.

I could never get her to go to a hospital when she was in need, so why would she go now? She would stop by Bo's sister's house to get updates and then stay for an hour or so and promptly go to the bar.

I sometimes brought books to read out loud to him. Anything to stimulate him back to health. I hung on to hope, though each day Linton struggled to function on his own. The medical team told us he could possibly be brain damaged, but they didn't know yet to what extent.

After two weeks the doctor asked to speak with us privately. "Mr. and Mrs. Logan, we have done multiple tests on Linton. His condition has worsened. This last test shows no brain activity at all. All his bodily functions are gone. He is basically staying alive through the machines. I hate to put you in this position, but it's time to decide if you want to take him off life support or put him in a rehab facility until he passes." The doctor who spoke looked at us sympathetically.

I felt the blood draining from my face. Never in my life had I thought I would have to face a decision like this. They left us alone in the room to talk it over.

Bo was totally distraught. "I can't do it. You must make this decision. You are the strong one."

I had hit my low point. *I am not the strong one. I am out of solutions.* A thought popped into my mind, and I walked out to where one of the doctors stood at the nurses' station.

"Do you have a priest or pastor on staff?" I asked.

"Oh, yes we do, Phylis. Do you want me to get him?"

"Yes. I can't make this decision without him." I paced up and down the hall, God in my thoughts. I needed to have someone of faith comfort me.

The priest walked in and shook our hands. He sat down and waited for our questions.

"Will my baby be blessed? Will he go to heaven? Should I keep him alive or take him off the machines?" I spit out the words like ammunition hitting a target.

Father Jack touched my hand. He must have noticed the fear in my face. "I can't make this decision. What if it's wrong?"

"I don't know what to do." Tears welled in my eyes.

"Phylis, let me help you. Here is what I can tell you. There are two parts of a person. The earthly body and the soul. Your son is an innocent baby. His body is his shell. It does the job it's supposed to do while he's here on earth. If he is meant to be here and to thrive, his body will do what it needs to stay alive. Right now the only thing that's keeping him alive is the machines. All the tests show there is no activity left for his body to survive. His soul is already with God. He is totally blessed. If God wants to perform a miracle, when you take him off the machines, his body will know what to do to stay alive. I hope this helps." He prayed with us.

His words comforted me, and when he left, I told the doctors to let me go home and think about it and I would give them an answer in the morning. Bo and I drove home, silent until we walked into our apartment.

"What do you think?" I looked at him as he sank down, distraught, on the couch.

"I . . . just . . . I . . . can't do it." He started to cry. "I'm leaving it up to you. You will make the right decision. I trust you." He rose and hugged me and went in the bedroom.

I sat silently and prayed. *Please let this be the right decision.*

The next morning the doctors and nurses were waiting to meet with us.

"We've made our decision. We are going to take him off life support. I don't want my son to suffer anymore." I was at peace.

I walked to the NICU room to be with Linton until they decided it was time.

The nurses there cried. "I'm so sorry, Phylis. We love Linton. I wish it could have been a different outcome."

I hugged each one and told them what a lifesaver they'd been. They showed Bo and me to a private room while we waited for them to prepare Linton. We would be able to hold him until he passed.

God must really hate me, I thought as I waited for the nurses to bring Linton to me. He knew I had taken a baby's life through abortion seven years before, so now He must be taking this one from me. That thing that *I would never have to think about again* reared its ugly head. We sat in that room, silent. Silent tears. Silent anguish.

They brought Linton to us, all bundled up like a newborn ready to be taken home. He was going home—just not the one I'd planned. I held him in my arms and told him how much he was loved. Bo cradled Linton's head, speaking the same words. We watched as he slowly breathed his last breath. As I looked down at his angelic face, a single tear rolled down his cheek. I gasped but didn't say anything. I looked at him and thought, *He is sad he's leaving us.* We held him until the end.

I was no longer a mom.

CHAPTER 11

New Beginnings

IT WAS TORTURE TO GO out in public—either people knew and treated us like we had an illness, or they didn't know, and then we were the bearer of bad news. The pain was too much to bear, and I wanted to die.

I was also at a crossroads. I had no job—I'd thought I was going to be a stay-at-home mom. I'd been miserable in my marriage before Linton's death, and his passing had compounded the wreckage. Each day started and ended the same. There was too much sadness between Bo and me.

"How was your day?" I'd try to muster up a happy face.

"Fine." Bo would walk past me to the bedroom to change out of his work clothes.

I didn't really care how his day was. I barely made it through without sobbing the day away.

He'd come out of the bedroom and grab something to eat. "I'm going over to Luke's house. I'll be back later." He'd peck me on the cheek and walk out.

I knew he was going to Luke's to get stoned. Getting high and drinking roared back into our lives to numb the pain. We barely spent any time together, and when we did, we fought through drunken pain and anger over the tragedy of our lives.

I sat at the kitchen table one day contemplating my next steps. The thought *What am I going to do* played over and over in my mind.

I put my head in my hands, and just as I started to say the words again, a voice said, seemingly out loud, *Start. Over.* I looked up from the table. No one was home. I walked to the front door. No one was there. I sat back down, and a weird sensation rippled through me. My thoughts were clear.

Something happened in that moment. Life had shifted. I knew what would happen if I stayed here with Bo. I would start drinking heavily. I would probably have an affair. I would implode my marriage.

I picked up the phone and called my friend Jessie. "I am leaving Bo. I need a place to stay and a job. Can you help me out?" I pleaded. Going back to my dad's wasn't an option because he didn't have the income to support both of us.

Jessie said, "Of course! You can stay at my place and sleep on the couch until you find your own apartment. It just so happens that we are hiring at my work. I can get you an interview tomorrow."

Since I couldn't face Bo pleading with me to stay, I wrote a letter telling him I wasn't coming back. I wanted out of this marriage for good this time. I didn't want anything from him except my furniture and clothes. I left my wedding ring on the table, packed a bag, and left.

I got the job at Pete's Produce Company on the spot. Staying at Jessie's, though, was difficult. She had a young son who didn't want us hanging out away from the apartment. We spent a lot of time at bars, and he got stuck at his grandmother's.

Though happy to be on my own, I was still processing my son's death. I masked the pain with alcohol and cocaine while I tried to figure out how I wanted my new life to look.

It helped that my new boss, Mr. Peters, understood my pain of losing a child, since he had gone through the pain of losing a teenage son years before.

"You have been so attentive to the details of the job. I'm proud of you for learning so fast, Phylis!" Walking by, he patted me on the shoulder.

I beamed with pride. I needed affirmations, and he spoke them at the right time.

Our small office of seven women and our boss was full of fun and laughter. Once a week, Mr. Peters would take us out for a leisurely lunch, which brought us closer, as we would share our personal lives with each other.

One morning, however, I came into work, depressed. I had been apartment hunting and had found the perfect place to live. The problem was, there were five other applicants. The chances of me getting this dream place would be slim to none. I flopped into my chair.

Mr. Peters swiveled his chair to face me. "What's wrong, sunshine? You aren't your bubbly self."

"Nothing. I'm fine." I kept typing so I didn't have to look at him.

"Join me in the conference room." He motioned for me to follow him.

Shoot. Am I in trouble? I should have come in with a better attitude. *Maybe he's mad at me.* I walked into the conference room and shut the door.

"Okay, it's just you and me. Tell me what's wrong. I see it all over your face."

Through my tears, I explained how I'd been sleeping on Jessie's couch. How I'd found the perfect apartment. How there were five applicants and I would never find another apartment like this one.

He asked me who the landlord was. I told him.

His lips curved into a big smile. "I know her. I can get you that apartment. Are you sure you want that one?" He held the phone to his ear.

My eyes widened. "Are you serious? I can't ask you to do that." Nothing like this happened to me.

He was already talking to her. "Hello, Diane? It's Ben. I have a very reliable employee here who applied for one of your apartments. I am vouching for her. Can she have it?" He was still smiling.

"Great. She will be over later today to give you the deposit and fill out the rest of the forms. Thanks so much." He set the phone onto its receiver. "It's yours."

I brought the last of my boxes into the apartment and then sat on the couch my dad had loaned me. I soaked in the beauty. The apartment was a cottage-style house split into four apartments. I had a cute little bedroom, a cozy living room, French doors that opened to a dining room, a balcony off the dining area, and a small kitchen perfect for one person. I could lay out in the private yard on sunny days.

I had gotten the rest of my furniture that had been left at the apartment Bo and I had shared. Bo had since moved back in with his mother.

I meandered from room to room, thankful for the blessing. I had a peace in my heart I hadn't felt before. I needed this alone time to mourn for my son, and I was realizing I didn't need a man in my life. I still had work to do on myself, but now I had time to think about my future.

CHAPTER 12

Light and Darkness

THE PRODUCE COMPANY HIRED MORE workers for the summer, and that was when Mike Mantelli breezed into the office one day to drop off his tags from the field. He was a good-looking college kid, and he had a soothing quality about him that made me smile. He was young though.

Mr. Peters, whom I now called Ben, decided to match us up.

"Hey, Mike. Are you going to our fundraiser this week?" Ben asked when Mike next showed up in the office.

"Oh, of course. Do you need me to bring anything?" He was always eager to please.

"Why don't you give Phylis a ride? She's going too. That way you don't have to take separate cars." He was grinning as I glared at him.

I quickly told Mike a ride wasn't necessary. He looked as if I'd hurt his feelings, so I backtracked and told him if he really wanted to, he could come pick me up.

During the drive to the fundraiser, I found out he was eight years younger than my twenty-seven-year-old self. Though I had had a great time with him that night and knew he was interested in me, I needed to be single for now. Mike was in college, an educated guy, but I was a newly separated mess.

We started off as friends. He would often call and ask if I wanted company, and our conversation was easy and filled with laughter. He would bring a pizza, beer, and sometimes flowers to my apartment, or we went to other social events together. He seemed older than most of the guys I had been with. He showed up on time when we met up, and he showed respect by leaving my apartment when it was time to go home.

I was in no rush to enter a bad relationship or marriage again, and I didn't need a man to make me happy. Once the summer was over, Mike would go back to school. I'd miss him.

He stopped by my apartment to say goodbye. "I know you said you didn't want anything serious. I thought I would be okay with that too, since I'm going back to school. I'm thinking, though, that maybe we could see each other on the weekends and any time I have a break. I really like you, Phylis." He stared at me with those puppy dog eyes.

I felt the same way. He had ignited something in me. Not only was he handsome, he was smart, funny, and steadfast in his dependability as a partner—so unlike any man I had ever met. I agreed we could try this new relationship.

"Phylis, I qualify for Social Security now," my mom said on the phone. "The only problem is, I need a permanent address. Then I would get my checks and apply for HUD housing so I could get my own apartment. Can I please come stay with you? Just for a month until I get on my feet again."

In theory it sounded great. She needed help with rides to the Social Security and HUD offices and with filling out forms. I'd let her stay with me so she could have an address. I clung to the hope that maybe she and I could finally have a healthy and happy relationship.

Shortly after moving in, she asked for extra money. She swore it was for food and toiletries. I gave her twenty dollars, and later that night, she came home drunk. She stumbled noisily into the house as I tried to sleep.

"Mom! Go to bed. I have to work in the morning." I was irritated.

"Dooon't talk to mee like that, youuung lady." She staggered her way to the couch and passed out.

I didn't pay much attention to what she was doing, as I was busy with my own social calendar and work. A few more weeks and she would be out of my hair.

I arrived home one day to find a neighbor waiting for me.

"Phylis, I hate to complain, but your mother . . . " He trailed off, looking upstairs. "She comes home in the middle of the day making all kinds of noise, and I think she ripped your curtains off the hinges today. I heard a big crash. If you look up at your window, half your curtain is down."

I apologized and let him know she would be leaving. I wouldn't let my mother ruin my life again. I raced upstairs. She paced back and forth in the living room.

"Where have you been? What happened? You can't come in here and ruin my apartment. The neighbors are complaining. I'm not getting kicked out because of you." I stood over her as she sat sank onto the sofa, shoulders stiff.

"I didn't do anything. Your neighbors are nosy. The curtains were an accident. Stop blaming me for everything." She stood her ground.

I'd heard it all before. "Get the hell out, Mom. I mean it. I don't care where you go—you are not welcome here. I have worked too hard for you to come here and ruin everything. I'm trying to improve my life. I wanted to improve yours. I guess that's not what you really want." I pointed to the door.

"You can't do that. I'm your mother. You should treat me with respect. You're going to take your neighbor's word over mine? You're in for a big shock when things don't go the way you think, missy."

Her words didn't scare me anymore. She was not going to ruin the peace I had created here. I stood there, arms crossed, waiting for her to take what little belongings she had and leave. She finally tossed a few items into her big tote purse, and then grabbed a paper bag in the kitchen for the rest.

She threw a last look my way. "You'll be sorry you did this. Just you wait. You will regret this. See if I care. Don't come crying to me when your life explodes in your face." She stomped out the door.

The air suddenly felt lighter. I didn't recognize how much stress she had put on me until she was gone.

I got my life back.

As much as I tried pushing Mike away in the beginning, he was not threatened by my independence, and he told me he would wait until I was ready. He had no hidden agenda—he just wanted me in his life.

Mike and I saw each other as much as we could while he finished school. We had been together for almost three years, and this relationship was the first one where I was content taking my time. I had shared all the mistakes of my past, and it didn't scare him away. I was met with compassion and a want to be there for me when I needed him. He wasn't closed off like the other men, and he shared every emotion as I experienced it.

He had met my mom and had seen her drunk, sober, and in her manic moods. He brought a calmness to Mom, who would become polite when he was around. "Mike, come sit here and tell me what's new with you." She'd smile wide, and he would sit and talk to her like she was his best friend.

We learned to set boundaries with her, and he encouraged me to take a stand and not let her push me around, but only respond to her "emergencies" when it really was important.

This time I was falling in love for good. I was having quiet prayers and conversations with God, asking Him to show me how to be a normal woman with a healthy relationship.

One Friday night, Mike drove down from school. He told me to get dressed up because he wanted to take me to a fancy dinner. But I wanted to go work out, yet he seemed insistent, so I hesitantly dressed into a silk flowery dress, and we were off.

"Where are we going? Can't we just eat locally? How far are we going? I'm not in the mood for being out too late. I had a hard day at work, and I'm tired." My questions and comments were curt.

Mike just laughed. "Stop being so nosy and relax. It's a surprise."

My mind flashed to an engagement ring. We had been talking about marriage now and then. He was nearly ready to graduate from college, and he wanted a future with me. I could picture my life with him forever.

I shook the thought out of my mind. It was probably just another fun dinner. I sat back and tried to enjoy the seventeen-mile drive through Pebble Beach. The ocean was breathtaking. It was a crisp night. We talked about all the gorgeous mansions we saw as we weaved down the winding road.

He stopped the car on a viewpoint. "Let's get out and look at the ocean. It's such a beautiful night." He walked around the back of the car to let me out, and we strolled to the edge.

The wind blew in a bit of a chill, and I turned to tell him we should go back to the car. He stood there with a black box open in his hand, revealing a stunning gold ring with a diamond.

"Phylis, I can't imagine my life without you. I love you so much. I will love you always. You have made me the happiest man. Will you marry me?" Tears filled his eyes as I nodded yes.

Tears welled in mine too. I honestly loved this man. We had been through some rough times in the three years we had been together, and we'd worked them out, as a good couple should.

Graduation day approached for Mike. I went with his family up to Santa Clara University to watch him accept his diploma. We celebrated all day and planned our wedding for the following year.

This was the family I'd always wanted.

CHAPTER 13

Finding My Jesus

I DIDN'T INVITE MY MOTHER to my wedding. She was still drinking and unstable. I didn't trust her to behave herself in front of the two hundred and fifty guests—I couldn't afford to have her make a fool of her and me.

She had moved into a studio apartment in town. I would sometimes see her walking back from the senior center with her weekly food bag. When I would drive by, she never looked up. By now I had been married a year, and I didn't want her drama in my life. It was easier to pretend she didn't exist.

Mike and I had our baby girl, Ariel, a few months after our first anniversary. She was perfect. It was a weird feeling being the mom instead of the daughter—a burst of joy as I held Ariel in my arms. A sadness that my own mother didn't have those feelings anymore, that maybe she never had.

I had the blessing of Mike's stepmother, Diana, to help me. She had come alongside me as my first mama mentor.

She showed me how to dress nicer. My clothes before I met her were mostly tight-fitting tops and jeans. She helped me with a more sophisticated look and taught me to cover up. My husband and I now attended black-tie events occasionally with his parents, as his dad was on the board of regents for Santa Clara University. My stepmother's help in picking out the perfect gowns were my favorite times with her. She mentored me to be a better woman.

Now she showed me how to be the best mom. She arrived each morning to help me with Ariel and let me get my rest. She would clean the house, do laundry, fend off too many visitors, and make us dinner. She'd then leave us with her home-cooked meal and return home for the night.

I observed how she talked with Ariel, the unconditional love she poured out. I wanted to aspire to that motherly role.

After a few months, I was on my own with my daughter. Diana still took Ariel for "grammy" visits almost every weekend so Mike and I could have alone time. I had returned to work, though it was difficult leaving her. I wanted to stay home and take care of her, but financially we weren't in that place yet. I liked where our life was headed though. We had bought our first home, and it felt like my life was falling into place.

Then came the fateful phone call. I had just walked through the door after picking up Ariel from daycare.

"Is this Phylis Mantelli?"

"Yes. Who is this?"

"This is South Valley Hospital. We have your mother, Ida Van Winkle, here. She was admitted last night with a broken hip. Unfortunately, she was drunk when she came in. We couldn't find out who to call to help her until this morning, when she could finally tell us. We found your phone number in her purse. We also couldn't give her any pain medication because she is inebriated. She has been screaming all night."

I hugged my daughter tight to me as my heart sank. This couldn't be happening. I hadn't thought about my mother in a year. My life was peaceful and easy, but if I chose to help her, it would get messy quick.

I was angry. There were three siblings in this family. Why was I the one she always called?

Then I heard a whisper. *I have chosen you. You are the one. Trust me.*

This was the journey I was on. It was time to mend this broken relationship with the mother who had never been there for me . . .

Mike lifted Ariel out of my arms, and I left for the hospital. I reluctantly entered the lobby. The elevator door opened, and I pressed the button for the second floor. As soon as I stepped into the hallway, I heard that familiar guttural screaming mixed with wailing and moaning.

The nurse caught my eye as I strode to the desk.

"Are you Mrs. Mantelli?" She spoke hesitantly, clearly hoping I was. She showed me the room where my mom lay in agony.

As soon as Mom saw me, she whimpered like a child. Her body relaxed for a moment because she knew someone was there who cared.

I didn't want to care. It would have been easier to tell the nurse who'd called that I couldn't help. "I'm here, Mom. Don't cry." I grabbed her hand and stroked her head. I didn't want to, but I felt sorry for her. The circumstances of how she'd landed here didn't matter. I knew she'd been drinking and had most likely fallen as a result. This was a replay of my life with her, yet my heart loved her anyway.

A nurse came in and informed me that Mom would have to be transferred to another hospital for surgery.

"No, Phylis. I don't want to go. I just want to go home. Take me home," she pleaded.

Knowing I couldn't fix her this time, I arranged for her transfer to the other hospital. She would then be taken to a rehabilitation facility for physical therapy. I followed her to make sure she was okay at the new hospital. She barely fussed, and the doctors operated the next day.

The move to rehab was not so easy. She fought it. "Why do I have to go there? Why can't you just take me home? You could take care of me just fine."

She couldn't comprehend how difficult a surgery she'd had. That this wasn't something she could heal quickly from and start walking again in a week.

When she finally settled into the facility, a nurse informed us about Mom's schedule. "We will have breakfast at seven thirty every morning. Here is your menu. You will get a chance to rest after that. Before lunch the physical therapist will work with you for about half an hour to start strengthening your legs so you can get back on your feet." She showed my mom the sheet of paper.

"What do you think, I'm stupid?" Mom barked back at her. "I know how to read this. And get back on my feet? I've been walking half my life. I'll get back on my feet. I don't need some stupid therapist to show me. I can do this myself."

"I'm so sorry," I said to the nurse. "Mom! Stop it. She is just doing her job. Don't yell at the messenger." I stood between my mom and the nurse, playing peacemaker.

Every day followed the same pattern. They would try to work with her. She would fight them. The therapist threatened to stop helping her. I told him that was exactly what she wanted. I worked around the appointments so I could be there during those times—that way I could help the therapist and keep my mom from being rude. She somehow listened to me when I scolded her for being so mean.

I couldn't wait until she could be on her own again.

Mom recovered quickly from her accident and returned home.

The doctor had tossed me a surprised glance. "We don't see this that often. Most patients in their seventies never fully recover to walk without any help of a cane or a walker."

I chalked it up to all those years of walking instead of driving. Her legs were strong. However, she required routine doctors' appointments, for which she needed rides. She also depended on me to take her to the grocery store—or whatever else she could think of to keep me close to her. I wanted my mom in my life. I wanted her to care about the person I had become. But the routine of taking care of her and my own household exhausted me.

I once brought Ariel over so Mom could enjoy her granddaughter. She swooned over her for the first few minutes. Then she turned the visit into a game to test me.

"I bet she's driving you crazy. I know how hard it is raising kids." She waited for me to agree with her.

"I get tired, but I'm just loving every minute of her growing up." I looked down at Ariel in my arms and smiled.

"Oh . . . just wait. You won't be as happy as time goes on. You think it's easy, but it's not. She will suck the energy out of you." She huffed at me like a wise old woman giving sage advice.

I didn't understand why Mom couldn't just be at peace. She could have been having the best time of her life. There was no man hurting her anymore. She had a place to live and enough money to get by, but she was still choosing to be miserable.

A few years later, Mike and I were thrilled to find out we were expecting our second child. We loved being parents. Our life together had been filled with challenges, and our relationship had grown deeper. I was discovering what commitment truly meant.

Something stirred in me, however. I thought about the last six years, how I had listened to a quiet voice to guide me. I had quit doing drugs, I had looked for healthy relationships, and my marriage to Mike was beautiful. But something was still missing.

It didn't feel right to return to my Catholic roots, though I was grateful my mom had at least instilled a modicum of faith in me. I'd felt God's presence all these years, and now I wanted to thank Him for my life. I also felt a need for him to bless this baby inside me.

The following week, my daycare lady told me she was going on vacation. She said not to worry—she had a backup person to watch all the kids.

"You went to high school with her. Her name is Lisa Grass," Susie told me when I picked up Ariel.

Lisa Grass . . . the friend who'd wanted to quit partying when she'd found out she was having a baby. "Oh wow! I haven't seen her in years. I can't wait to talk to her."

I went by Lisa's the next week, and we giggled and hugged each other. Our conversation lasted longer than the typical drop-off for my girl. Each day when I picked Ariel up, Lisa invited me to stay and talk. I found out she had become a Christian many years ago. I was curious, so I asked her questions about her faith. I explained to her that I wanted to protect this baby I was carrying. I wanted God's blessing. I just didn't know what church I wanted to go to.

"Oh, Phylis. I have the perfect church for you. They are having a children's Christmas play this weekend. You must take Ariel. She will love it."

That following Sunday, Ariel and I went to the church—Mike had refused to join us. I walked in with Ariel and was instantly greeted by two women. They showed me to a seat in the front row. I was not prepared for what I saw and heard—people talking and laughing. Growing up, there was never laughter in church. That would have been frowned upon.

The children were adorable, and Ariel loved it. After the kids' play, the pastor came out to deliver a short sermon. I listened to his words, which resonated with me. He talked about having a peace like no other with a God who loved us.

"Friends, I want you to know that especially during this time of year, there are many people who don't feel the joy of our loving God. He loves you. He wants you to be close to him. He wants you to reach out to him. Pray, praise, and let other Christians surround you with love during this Christmas season." He ended the sermon with a prayer.

A longing stirred deep inside my soul. Shaking, I began to cry. God had been with me the whole time. He was waiting for me. I asked Him to bless this second baby. I prayed for my family. I had come home—a home no one could drag me away from, not even the devil himself.

CHAPTER 14

The Unraveling

"CHURCH IS GREAT FOR YOU, honey. I'm not there yet. I won't be going to church with you," Mike had flatly told me after I started attending worship services.

Those words had been my first test of faith, and I'd failed badly. Angry with God, I'd wondered why he would bring me this far only to disappoint me.

The one thing that had kept me coming back to church were the people. They had become a family. When I had a problem, they would talk to me and pray for me. I leaned on my faith, though I didn't always understand it.

Now, three and a half years later, I was still attending church with my daughters. Ariel and Dominique, seven and four years old, watched as their dad stayed home while I took them to church by myself. But when I traveled out of town, they missed Sunday school and children's church, because their dad usually took them out for brunch.

When in Chicago at a conference for my direct-sales business, I had finished a Sunday meeting and called home to check in.

"Hey, girls. I miss you guys. How's it going?" They were both listening on the other line.

"Mom! Guess what we did this morning?" I heard the excitement in Ariel's voice.

"What, baby?" I figured Mike had taken them out for a special breakfast.

"Dad took us to church! He woke us up and said we were going," she proudly told me.

I mouthed *Oh my gosh!* to my roommate, who was watching me. She smiled at me, understanding I had just received good news. She had no idea how good this news was.

After that, Mike slowly eased into attending with us, until it became routine. God was showing me he could deepen my marriage bond.

He was also working on my relationship with my mother.

Once she could walk again, Mom had returned to her old ways. She currently lived above a bar. She could walk downstairs any time of the week and have a few drinks. I tried to keep her healthy by bringing good food to her. I introduced her to new activities that didn't include alcohol, but she never connected with other people unless they were partiers. At one point I convinced her to try an alcohol rehab facility.

She lasted one week and left. "I am not like *those* people. I am not an alcoholic. I can stop any time I want. I don't even drink that much. Remember, I don't even keep alcohol in the house. How can I have a problem?" Her excuses poured out one after another.

Over the years it had been a battle to love her as the person she was. My girls, now teens, had long asked not to visit her. They'd seen right through her. They weren't used to cruel words, and they didn't want me to hear them either. I assured them that I didn't take them to heart, but I wanted to respect their grandmother even when it was difficult. I explained that she was deep-down lonely.

Mom got drunk again one night and broke her other hip when she slipped in the lobby of her apartment. The apartment manager, who I'd become friends with, kept an eye on Mom and told me she'd been rushed to the hospital.

This time the hip did not heal as well. Mom was older and even more stubborn. She refused to do her workouts. Scared of falling again, she wouldn't leave the house. Or her favorite chair.

"Mom, let's take a walk. Just around the apartment. We don't even have to go downstairs. We can walk around up here." I grabbed her hands to help her up.

She was sore and weak. "I can't walk far. It's too hard." She hesitantly took hold of me.

We walked around for about ten minutes, then she went back to her chair and watched Jerry Springer while I made her lunch. We did this several times a week. This strong-willed woman who used to walk everywhere wanted to stay home out of fear of falling again.

During one visit, I noticed that her feet looked swollen and red. I lifted her pant leg. Her legs were covered with raw open wounds. She'd never told me.

"Mom! What is going on? We need to take you to the doctor right away. This is serious." I picked up the phone to make an appointment.

"No, no . . . just put some lotion on them. They're fine."

I saw the fear in her face, but I no longer listened to her pleas. I wouldn't be playing nursemaid to her. I took her to the doctor, who said she had serious infections on her legs, caused by her sedentary life. They told me how to take care of her, and they assigned a visiting nurse to show me how to apply the medications.

The nurse showed up at mom's apartment the next day. She instructed me on how to glove up, soak Mom's feet in the plastic tub, dry them gently, rub medication cream on her legs up to her knees, and then wrap them up in gauze. I did this every other day.

I was doing just that when my mom looked down at me one day. I knelt by her feet, putting my gloves on next to the tub of warm water. As I gently lifted her feet into the tub, she patted the top of my head.

"You are a good daughter, and I bet you are a good mom." She continued to stroke my head.

My world stopped.

Words of affirmation from my mom as I knelt beside her, washing her feet. I was aware that God knew I needed to hear those words.

The last few months had been hard. She had been especially cruel with her words and behavior. I would set her up for the day, then leave as soon as I could to get away from the negativity. I would get to my car and argue with God. *Why can't you just take her? She hates this world. She is a miserable human being. I don't want to do this anymore.* I would hear a whisper in my head. *Patience and grace, patience and grace.* I didn't have either.

Now as she sat before me, I almost backed away from the shock of her words. God told me to soak them in. I was a grown woman. I was a mom, a wife, a sister, a daughter. I needed to hear them. I looked up at her face. It was soft and gentle. We smiled at each other.

"Thanks, Mom." I teared up and continued to clean her wounded legs.

After seeing the girls off to school, I walked up the stairs to Mom's apartment. As usual, she was sitting in her chair. Next to her on the side table was the Kleenex box. Beside the box were all the tissues perfectly folded and stacked, like a tissue tower.

"What is this?" I laughed, thinking it was a joke.

She looked over, shocked. "Who did this? I didn't do this!"

I thought she was kidding, but she honestly didn't know. I teased her about it that day.

Then she would leave refrigerated food out all night. The stove would burn the pot still on it. A note would be left by a downstairs neighbor that Mom had made noise at two in the morning—they wanted her to stop walking around all night and stop slamming cupboards.

Mom was not herself. She'd forget dates and memories. She'd forget to take her medication. I would write it out for her and leave just the right amount. The next day I would find the pills still sitting on her dish.

"I saw them, but I thought I had already taken them. I thought these were for today." She seemed beyond confused.

We talked to the doctor at her next appointment. He told me she might be experiencing some signs of dementia. He wanted me to keep an eye on her. He would send the visiting nurse to check on her from time to time.

Months later I arrived home after making Mom lunch and setting her up for the day. I had a full schedule of work from home. I had booted up my computer, when the phone rang.

"Phylis! Where have you been?" Mom screamed at me.

"What are you talking about? I was there this morning. I just left you."

"Stop lying to me. I haven't seen you in two weeks!"

"Mom . . . check the fridge. There is a ham and cheese sandwich in there. I made lunch." Now I was worried.

She was disoriented. I told her I'd stop by later and hung up. I made a call to the nurse to let her know what happened.

"We may have to think about putting her in a nursing facility. She is going to need extra help that you can't give," the nurse informed me.

That decision was made for me a few weeks later.

"Pat was taken to the hospital. We had to call 911. She was standing naked in the hallway screaming that someone was attacking her," said the manager of Mom's apartment building.

I rushed to see her.

She had no recollection of what had happened. "I want to go home. They can't make me stay here. I'm fine." She pushed at her blankets as she lay in the hospital bed.

I talked to the nurse who had been visiting her weekly. The nurse told me we could get her in the same facility where she had gone after her hip surgeries. They had an opening. Mom was bumped up on the list since she was a danger to herself.

I had to make the decision that day or lose the spot, but I didn't want to put her in a nursing home. *This is too much for me to handle on my own, but I need to let them to do it. Things are unraveling fast.*

CHAPTER 15

You're a Good Daughter

MOM WAS CRYING. SHE DIDN'T want to be there. I had met with the doctors, nurses, and therapists, who had prepared me. They told me what to say and how to respond to her questions and comments.

I settled her in with some of the comforts from her home. I brought her favorite blanket, some pictures of her grandchildren, and some magazines. I bought her flowers to set on her nightstand.

Mom wept as I helped her into the bed. "Why can't I go home? They are crazy. I'm the normal one. Please let me go home."

"Mom, it's not up to me. As soon as the doctors tell me it's okay, then I will take you home, all right?" I explained it just like the doctors had told me. It seemed to appease her.

I visited her every day. I wanted to make sure the nurses were taking good care of her. I needed her to know I wasn't abandoning her.

I made friends with a couple of the nurses, one of which was a woman who went to the same church as I did. We saw each other at service every Sunday. She took special care of Mom when she was on shift, and I trusted Troy Ann with my mom. There was one other nurse who

Mom loved. Of course, he was a male nurse. His name was Aiden, and Mom wore the biggest smile on her face when he came in to tend to her.

"He's so nice and very handsome," Mom gushed.

Aiden laughed and looked over at me. "I love your mom. She is so sweet."

I laughed because "sweet" was not a word I would have used to describe my mom. She had been on medication since she'd arrived, which seemed to steady her demeanor.

One morning I walked toward her room, when I was stopped by the therapist on staff. Julie Venet was someone I had talked to often when Mom first arrived. She'd given me comfort and good advice. She asked to speak to me in private in her office.

"I noticed you are here every day." She leaned over her desk. "You know you don't have to come every day to see your mom, right?"

"Well, I want to make sure she doesn't think I just dumped her here and forgot about her." *Did I do something wrong?*

"Phylis, I am releasing you from all this guilt. You brought your mom here so we could take care of her. Let us do our jobs. You have been a very good daughter. Most people don't even visit their loved ones ever. You have taken such good care of her for sixteen years. It's your time to go and live your life. You can see her anytime you want. Just don't feel like you have to be here every day and micromanage everything." She sat back.

I erupted into tears. I appreciated her words. It had become such a habit to feel like Mom's protector. It was hard to pass the baton to someone else. We chatted for a while, and without realizing, I was receiving therapy.

I still visited Mom a few times a week. Some days were better than others. She would be content and looking out her window, with her favorite TV show playing in the background. Other days were rough.

I heard Mom screaming one day as I entered her room. The nurses were trying to get her into the bathroom to change her. She grabbed the sides of the door and kicked and screamed.

"Hey! What's going on? Mom! Calm down." I touched her arm to assure her I was there.

She pulled away from me and kept screaming.

"We've been trying to get her in here to change her diaper. She's scheduled to take a shower too." The nurses seemed frustrated as they tried to pull her into the bathroom.

"Guys, can you give her a minute? You are making her more anxious. I will try to calm her down, and we can try again." I wrapped an arm around Mom and walked her back to bed.

She looked at me, confused. I helped her lay down and watched her as she flipped through the TV channels.

"It's okay, Mom. They just want to change you and make you clean." I patted her hand and gazed into her eyes, wondering what was going on inside her head, since she couldn't describe it. She eventually told me she would take her shower, and I called for the nurses.

On another afternoon I found her in the room next door. She was in her wheelchair, talking to another lady.

"She's my friend." Mom pointed to the lady.

That was a good day for Mom, as were the days when she got her hair done by visiting hair stylists, when the lunchroom had music, and when the facility had bring-your-animals-to-work day. Mom loved petting the dogs, and came alive on those days, and her verbal skills were more active.

I consulted with Julie, and she would update me—she and I had an easy sisterhood. Julie let me know that my mom was progressing faster than most with her type of dementia. She informed me that hospice would be taking over to help Mom through her final days. I was grateful for Julie's help.

I watched Mom go from different moods and emotions to being quiet and somber. She sat in her wheelchair all day and stared out the window or watched TV. She never left her room anymore except to take showers. Birds and deer often passed by the big square window by her bed. She used to get excited to see all the wildlife. Now she didn't respond.

I stopped in one day for a quick visit in between my errands. I hadn't been seeing her as often because she didn't talk much. I walked in and found her in front of the TV.

"Hey, Mom. How are you?" I patted her hand.

She jerked away and threw me a dirty look.

I sat down on her bed. "Mom . . . do you know who I am?" I drew out the words.

She shook her head no.

My heart dropped. She stared right through me.

The mom I knew was gone.

There would be no more reminiscing. No more laughter or the little banter we engaged in.

I sat there on her bed pretending to watch TV with her. She never took her eyes off me. She said nothing. It grew so uncomfortable, I wanted to cry. I watched the clock in her room, waiting for twenty minutes to pass.

"Well, I'll see you later, okay?"

She kept staring at me as I backed out of her room.

The nurses were at their stations. "How's Pat today? She's been really quiet."

"She doesn't know who I am." I waited for some explanation.

"Yeah. We were seeing the same thing. I'm sorry, Phylis. This is part of the process. She's not in any pain. We are taking good care of her, sweetie."

I staggered outside and sat in my car, bursting into sobs. This woman who had given me nothing but grief for most of my life was breaking my heart. I thought I would be ready for this day. I wasn't. I called my sister and told her that Mom's time was running out. If she wanted to see Mom and say her piece, she had to come soon. My brother had already visited a few times.

I wanted more time. She had been calmer here. I was on a good schedule with her, and I had my freedom, knowing she was safe and taken care of.

It would be awkward visiting someone who didn't recognize me. This was going to be rough.

A few weeks later Mom went into a coma. She shook violently and looked tortured. I called my church and asked if Pastor Tom, our worship leader, would come and say prayers over her. I sang with him at church, so we had developed a friendship. I had watched him preside over funerals. He was soft spoken and gifted in helping those in need.

We met in Mom's room. She shook so hard that her bed vibrated. Pastor Tom and I started praying over her. Halfway through the prayer, Mom took a huge gasp of air and then went quiet. We kept praying. I was afraid to open my eyes. *Did she just pass?* I slowly opened my eyelids. Pastor and I looked at each other.

Mom was calm and breathing evenly.

"I thought she died!" I laughed awkwardly.

"Me too!" He laughed with me.

We watched her sleep, peaceful. I knew what that gasp was. I suspected Mom had accepted the Holy Spirit into her heart. It was like seeing two different people. She had been struggling when we had arrived. Now she was calm. I thanked Pastor Tom for his beautiful prayer.

My sister came the next day. Her tears flowed enough to fill a river. So much time had passed between them. Their relationship had been strained over the years. It was the same with my brother. They couldn't get past her hard surface, and I couldn't blame them. The only thing left was goodbyes. We would never be able to fix anything that had broken all those years ago.

Another day passed. I was alone with Mom. Hospice told me she had about twenty-four hours left. There was one more thing left.

I stroked her hair as I bent down and whispered, "Mom, you can go now. I forgive you. I'm okay. I'm happy, and I have a good life."

I kissed her forehead. I sat down and opened my Bible. I watched her sleeping and wondered if she saw Jesus. Outside, two deer stood right by her window. One was eating. The other looked at me and stepped toward me, gazing into my eyes intently. We stayed like this for a few minutes. He was so majestic that I wondered if he was there to guide my mom to heaven. We spoke a silent language. Knowing she was leaving this earth, I wanted to stay and spend the night, so I sat in the big green chair and kept reading.

In the next bed, her roommate was talking to her stuffed bear. I tried to focus and read, but the delusional roommate's voice grew louder. I thought if she would settle down, I could sleep here tonight. I wanted to be here when Mom passed. The lady spoke louder and louder. I couldn't do it. I promised myself that I would go home, get a few hours of sleep, and come back early in the morning.

At six o'clock the next morning, the phone rang.

I knew who it was.

"Mrs. Mantelli?"

"Yes?" I didn't want to hear the words.

"I'm so sorry to tell you. Your mom passed away a half hour ago. We have called the coroner. You can come by any time after they're done."

I hung up the phone. It was just like Mom. She didn't want me there. She left the way she wanted.

At Mom's funeral, I met second cousins I had heard of but never met. The word had spread about her passing. Aunt Laura came. She had finally become a mom years ago. The doctors had told her it was impossible, but she'd given birth to a beautiful baby girl. My cousin Brooke was grown now, but I thought about God's miracles. When people said things were impossible, God made them possible.

Aunt Laura and I reminisced. "Oh, Philly, your mom was a pistol." My aunt looked at my mom in the casket. "Patty girl, I will miss you."

It was comforting to see people who loved Mom. Friends from our church came to pay their respects, as did coworkers. The day was beautiful and blessed with people who loved us.

My family gathered around me. Mike wanted to protect me from my sorrow. My youngest daughter, Dominique, was my comforter that day. I watched my twelve-year-old daughter work the crowd. She was the perfect young lady as she talked to relatives and friends she had never met. She comforted me with hugs and stayed close, in case I needed her.

But Ariel was shellshocked. She stayed in the back of the room, nervous and uncomfortable.

I gave my eulogy, trying to stay as truthful about Mom as I could. "Thank you all for coming today to say goodbye to my mom. She was the mother of three children, seven grandchildren, and two great-grandchildren. To say my life with my mom was an adventure is an understatement! She was definitely a challenge, and today I want to tell you about the things I've learned from her.

"My mom loved anything to do with the arts, including singing and dancing, and many of her granddaughters have acquired this love too, three of them being on competitive dance teams.

"Something I learned about her this last year was that my mom wanted to write a book about her life. She had some titles picked out and wrote a few notes to start. I too love to write and perhaps will fulfill that dream for her someday.

"Something that was a surprise for me was that my mom was a spiritual woman. I found many letters and notes from people thanking her for her words of encouragement and prayers for them.

"The things that I see of my mom that live on in all her children, grandchildren, and great-grandchildren are big brown eyes, great smiles, quick wit, and great strength.

"I have learned from my mom that even in the bad times, I can learn a lesson. So today, Mom, I say 'thank you' for the journey. We made it through, and I hope your next life is filled with hope, joy, and peace, and that I get to see that next time."

We concluded the services, and Kecia stayed behind to sit by Mom's coffin while I went outside to give people directions to the reception.

The funeral worker informed me they needed to put my mom in the car to take her to the burial site but that my sister wouldn't let them. I walked back inside. Kecia sobbed uncontrollably, hugging the coffin. "I can't let her go. I can't."

With my mama's heart, I walked up to my baby sister and hugged her tight. "Sissy, we have to go. You need to let them take her. Everyone is waiting." I gently pulled her away.

Kecia would always be my first baby.

CHAPTER 16

The Next Generation

THE GIRLS GRADUATED FROM COLLEGE. Mike and I became empty-nesters. Life was full and always an adventure.

I had co-led several Bible studies over the years. Each time I shared my story about my difficult relationship with Mom, afterward a young girl would ask if we could meet. They were struggling in their relationships with their moms also. I would mentor them for a few months. More girls would come. I was scheduling dinner dates and coffee dates whenever I could fit them in. God showed me that he uses our stories and pain for good.

The fear that I wouldn't be a good mom had disappeared. I had watched my own daughters grow up into independent, beautiful, spiritually grounded young women. It hadn't come easy. They had gone through their own struggles. We had survived as a family, and I loved my girls with all my heart. They loved me too. We weren't perfect. Sometimes cruel words crept in, but we quickly apologized and found a way back to each other. They knew our home was their safe haven. Any of their friends were welcome anytime. We took in people when there was a need. God had blessed me with a fulfilling life—in spite of how it started out.

Ariel was getting married. She had dated Julius for six years. He was perfect for her, and we loved him so much. She wanted to get married in three months. I thought it was impossible. But my daughter was different from me. She was focused and confident. I helped with the things I was good at—invitations, picking out a dress. She did everything else, with Julius by her side. They were a team.

The wedding day dawned with blue skies. We all gathered at a beautiful hotel in San Diego, where the ceremony would take place. I watched both my daughters from afar. I felt my heart explode with love for them as they giggled together and shared sister moments.

All I ever wanted in life was to be a good mom. I never had big career goals. I simply wanted to change the generational dysfunction I had grown up in.

Mike and I waited by the stairwell for our turn to walk down the aisle. I started bawling the minute I saw Ariel in her dress. The wedding march started, and I rose from my seat and watched my husband proudly walk his baby girl down the aisle. The tears flowed again. Just then I heard the heart-whispered words: *patience and grace, patience and grace.*

These words struck me like lightning—those were the words God had told me that day when I was frustrated with my mom. I thought he'd given me those words to get me through the rough days with her. I now understood that *patience and grace* were words for this present time.

God was showing me that he wanted me to be patient. There were good things coming. He wanted me to have grace. He would bless me with a bigger family and more love. He knew the desires of my heart.

I just had to follow the path he had for me. The road had been long. Filled with loss and disappointments. Life got messy. It wasn't perfect.

There would be many chapters in my life that would still be challenging, but God's unfailing love would never change. I only had to lean on His promises, act on the whispers He would give me each morning.

I thought about my mom, and prayed she was smiling down on a daughter who never gave up.

Order Information

To order additional copies of this book, please visit
www.redemption-press.com.
Also available on Amazon.com and BarnesandNoble.com
Or by calling toll free 1-844-2REDEEM.

CPSIA information can be obtained
at www.ICGtesting.com
Printed in the USA
BVHW080335030919
557364BV00007B/899/P